Unemployment in Assam

An Account of Human Error

UNEMPLOYMENT IN ASSAM

An Account of Human Error

BHAKTA DAS

COSMO PUBLICATIONS
NEW DELHI 1992

Printed in India
First Published 1992

UNEMPLOYMENT IN ASSAM: AN ACCOUNT OF HUMAN ERROR

ISBN NO. 81-7020-574 3

Published by
RANI KAPOOR (Mrs.)

COSMO PUBLICATIONS
For Genesis Publishing Pvt. Ltd.
24-B, Ansari Road, Darya Ganj
New Delhi-110 002, INDIA.

Typeset at ADR Enterprises, New Delhi
Printed at Mehra Offset Press, Delhi

The Memory of
My Father and Mother

Foreword

According to Assam Government sources the total number of job seekers registered with the Employment Exchanges was put at 9.77 lakhs at the end of December, 1989. Of this, number of educated job seekers was 5.52 lakhs. This project the enormity of the problem of unemployment of our State.

Shri Bhakta Das, Joint Secretary to the Government of Assam, Education, has made a successful attempt to deliberate on this very important problem confronting the State. It should be appreciated that as a conscientious Officer, Shri Das could find time to study the background, causes and magnitude of the unemployment problem with revealing statistics. As Director of the Employment and Craftsman Training, Shri Das had the opportunity of looking at the problem from close quarters. Shri Das has also reviewed the functioning of the Employment Exchanges and the University Employment Bureaus of the State.

I am sure the book will help the administrators and the planners in formulating policies to meet the challenge of unemployment and also provide adequate background material to research scholars to undertake study on the subject.

I congratulate Shri Das for his commendable work.

N.K. CHOUDHURY
Vice-Chancellor
Gauhati University

Preface

Even after three decades of planning employment opportunities have become an illusion to the Assamese people. Unemployment has become a real problem due to the growth of population, lack of growth of Industries, lack of entrepreneurship and shyness of capital. The increase in the population is though the result of increase in the birth rate and decrease in the death rate, but the illegal immigrants is the main factor and this illegal immigration is the deep-rooted malaise in Assam. Schemes on self-employment are expected to bring ray of hope to the young talents who are now in turmoil in Assam.

There are thousands of unemployed people in Assam, where the 1st Oil Refinery of the world was set up. The result is the growing discontentment among the employable educated youth, anger, frustration and damage has already been done to the psychological fabric of the Assamese youth.

The publication of this book "Unemployment in Assam: An Account of Human Error", I hope will throw some light on the causes of unemployment in Assam. In this Book I have discussed about the Employment service in South-East Asian countries also. The volume also contains information about employment situation and employment service in India and Assam alongwith the programmes implemented by the Government so far, to create employment. I have also discussed in this volume about the measures to be taken to solve the problem of unemployment in Assam. The information given in this book with datas will be of help to planners/researchers and policy-makers. I hope this book will be welcomed by the readers.

I am grateful to Shri N.K. Chaudhury, Vice-Chancellor of Gauhati University, who has kindly gone through the manuscript and gave me valuable advice and encouragement for its publications. I am also thankful to my publisher for publishing this book, and to my wife and sons, who have encouraged me to take up this work.

BHAKTA DAS

Contents

Contents

[illegible] of employment [illegible]

Employment [illegible]

Employment and [illegible]

Employment situation and [illegible]
[illegible]

A [illegible] of the [illegible]
[illegible]

[illegible] by the [illegible]
Employment [illegible] During [illegible]
[illegible]
Employment

[illegible]

CHAPTER 1

Causes of Unemployment in Assam

Assam have crossed over three decades of planning but the problem of unemployment could not be solved. Whatever employment would be generated have been neutralised by the release of manpower in the employment market due to growth of population, rapid expansion of educational facilities, handicapped by lack of growth of industries, lack of entrepreneurship and shyness of capital. Whenever and whatever opportunity comes, outsiders avail the opportunity depriving the sons of the soil, though the young Assamese generation is equally intelligent and capable and quite at par with their outsider counterparts.

As per 1971 Census, Assam has a population of 146 lakhs representing 34.95 per cent growth rate against all India average at 24.80 per cent during the period 1961-1971.

The projected population of Assam as on 1st March, 1988 was 244.31 lakhs which indicates increase of 98.43 lakhs people over that on 1971. This increase in the population is the root cause to aggravate the employment problem in Assam. As per the projection, the population in the age-group 15-59 years was 104.05 lakhs in 1981 which will increase to 143.13 lakhs on 1st March, 1991.

This shows an addition of 39.07 lakhs of population in the age-group 15-59 years by 1st March, 1991. At this rate, 20 lakhs of people will be added to the labour force which will create the unemployment in Assam more acute.

The increase in the population is though the result of increase in the birth rate and decrease in the death rate, but incoming of Bangladeshies, is the main factor. Immigration from Bangladesh is at its peak. More people from Bangladesh are taking up residence in the forests of Assam. Because the Bangladeshies are dependant mainly on agriculture and Assam being a platform just above three feet of the sea water level and land being fertile, attracts the hard working Bangladeshies. The local Assamese farmer do not know how to get maximum water by utilising minimum finance. There is lack of knowledge amongst the Assamese farmers, the benefit that they will get by utilising the scientific method of cultivation for increasing food production. There is lack of storage facilities, lack of credit facilities in the rural sector. The Assamese farmers are handicapped by these constraints for years, did not cultivate the lands in the forest areas. The Bangladeshies exploited the situation and occupied all vacant forest land and the Char and Grazing areas. Gradually the cultivable land have become scarce to Assamese farmers.

The problem of illegal immigration is the deep rooted malaise in Assam. The people of Assam is no longer enthused about the cause of illegal immigration from earstwhile East Pakistan which had inflammed them to revolt for six years. Even after formation of the Assam Gana Parishad Government in Assam nothing have been done to resolve the actual problem. Nothing have been done to move in the direction of sending away the illegal immigrants from Assam and the unemployment problem in Assam is growing more and more as the effect of this continuing and untreated Cancer. Mr. C.S. Multan the then Census Superintendent in his report—1931 said, "It is sad but by no means improbable that in another 30 years Sibsagar District will be the only part of Assam in which Assamese will find themselves at home." Thus incoming of unlawful settlers in Assam has been a trial for the provincial Government since 1918.

This problem assumed serious proportion on account

of the large influx of immigrants in 1944-45. In the Census of 1961 the all India percentage increase of population was 21.64 per cent. For the same decade population increased in Assam by 34.98 per cent. The Census of 1971 saw an all India increase of population of 24.8 per cent. In the case of Assam it was again 34.90 per cent. Much more disturbing is the case of Karbi Anglong and North Cachar Hills Districts. The percentage growth rate mentioned below from the Census reports of 1951 onwards shows how alarming is the situation.

	1951	*1961*	*1971*
Karbi Anglong	30.06	79.21	63.28
North Cachar	6.16	36.95	40.00

The Chief Election Commissioner during the conference of Electoral Officers held in 1978 observed that the influx has become a regular feature and that the increase in population which is likely to be recorded in 1991 Census would be more than 100 per cent over the 1961 Census. A stage would be reached when Assam will have to reckon with the foreign nationals which will constitute a sizeable percentage. If not, the majority population in the State. The fact that a large number of immigrants succeeded in illegally coming to Assam and settling down unnoticed, proves that the measures so far taken have not been effective and the basic idea that land is the central core for their existence to the Assamese people, their future, the future of their progeny, jobs, employment opportunities has become an illusion to the Assamese people and today Assam has become an account of human error compounded by arrogant and immatured decisions.

This have further been aggravated by fresh influx of Bangladeshies and high birth rate among them. The population in Assam have increased alarmingly and it has now on the one hand become difficult for an Assamese farmer to get sufficient land to engage him and his children fully in Agriculture and whatever land they have, they cannot cultivate the same for the whole year fully, due to successive floods in the summer and scarcity of water in the winter. The stage has come when the Assamese farmer can engage himself and his children only 120 days in a year in his land. The rest of the days in a year, they remain idle and this has resulted in the unemployment in the villages, yielding on rush of young villagers to the towns seeking employment. The number of job seekers through employment exchanges of the State went up by 2.8 per cent between January and September, 1988.

Agriculture in Assam which is the main economic activity is characterised by monocropping and high risk of flood, low productivity and very poor extension and support system. It is gradually becoming less attractive and the rural youth is running after white-collar jobs. The rural youth feel that farming is not viable and cannot sustain them. They feel helpless because of their lack of skills that can fetch them alternative appointment. Today for the youth in Assam on the one side there is an increase in the cost of living and lack of alternatives on the other. Though a few industrial projects are being set up but it will take a long time before the impact on the rural population will be seen. The Assamese rural youth have not been able to find employment in the projects except in Grade IV services like peon, driver etc. for lack of suitable skills. Thus the large industries like Oil Refinary/Paper Mill is not a solution to rural unemployment.

On 31.12.89 the live registers of employment exchanges which covers only a segment of the unemployed persons had 977126 lakhs registered unemployed in the State of Assam of whom 552215 lakhs are educated unemployed. For solving the unemployment problem the State Government should set up rural industries to give adequate employment avenues and to stop the mobility of skilled and semi-skilled workforce from the rural to urban areas.

In Assam, the number of unemployed persons is increasing gradually not only among workers but also among the educated middle class. Unemployment leads to poverty. Unemployment and poverty are not only bad but it degenerates man to less than human being and if this trend is allowed to continue, it will jeopardise the economy and it will lead to explosive situation of grave consequences.

The projected present population in Assam is about 243 lakhs. 90 per cent of this population i.e. 219 lakhs lives in villages. In towns, only 44 lakhs people live. For the villages, agriculture is the only employment source. But only 36 lakhs persons are engaged in agriculture out of 219 lakhs which indicates that 6 persons depends on the income of only one person in the villages. As such the unemployment problem in the rural sector is more serious, but we are not so serious about this problem in the rural sector. It is estimated that the number of employable unemployed in the villages of Assam will be approximately 70 lakhs i.e. one-third of the rural population. There is one another field which can absorb the candidates for white-collar jobs i.e. in the Government and semi-Government offices. The educational system which has stimulated a large production of graduates and masters have swelled the number of educated unemployed in Assam. Competition among too many aspirants struggling for few jobs is leading to frustration and the educated unemployed have developed revolutionary instinct.

One peculiar characteristic of Assamese Society is the existence of various social groups whose adult members only do certain types of works. As a result of spread of education, more people are joining the ranks of those who go for white-collar jobs only.

Labourers are to be brought from far away places like Bihar to do earth work on road and irrigation projects. Even in the case of the crash programmes for employment which sought to provide employment to rural unskilled youths in their own villages, it has been found that in the off seasons also, only a few persons report for work though a large number of people remain unemployed or underemployed in the neighbourhood. Which indicates that people are not availing themselves of these opportunities in full, in spite of unemployment and underemployment being rampant.

The authorities have not been able to detect and deport the foreigners as per Assam Accord. After going through the I.M.D.T. Act., 1983 one can easily realise that it would not be easy to deport the lakhs of foreigners illegally staying in Assam unless this act is repealed. The Union Minister for Law and Justice, late Dinesh Goswami on 26th August, 1990 while addressing a workers meeting of the A.G.P. at Rabindra Bhawan, Guwahati stated that the Illegal Migrants Determination Tribunal Act (I.M.D.T.) 1983 could not be repealed, (Source: *Assam Tribune,* dt. 27th August, 1990). The Assam Accord signed on Aug. 15, 1985 did not therefore fulfill the purpose for which the people faced the bullets and many of them became martyrs.

Though Assam is rich in oil, but the crude oil of Assam has been pumped out of the State to feed a bigger refinery located at Barauni in Bihar. Even for the Toy refinery at Noonmati (Gauhati) the Assamese people had to launch a movement. Assam produces tea, but all the major offices of the Tea Board have been functioning from West Bengal. Major industries remain still a far cry in Assam as necessary infrastructures have not been created for growth of industries in Assam during the 42 years of independence. Assam remained neglected due to the weak leadership. The State though rich in natural resources but the job generating industries are conspicuous by their absence in the State.

Again there is the problem of migration of the rural educated youth to the towns in search of white collar jobs. While the urban sector is facing the challenge of providing white collar jobs to the educated, the rural sector is facing the problem of landless farmers/workers, marginal farmers, rural artisans, fishermen, etc.

In the Urban sector the tendency amongst the unemployed youths is to run after jobs from office to office. The white collar jobs being limited, most of them remain unemployed and continue to inflate the number of unemployed. A strong feeling has developed that the young boys and girls leaving—schools, colleges and universities regards manual work and vocational employment as something inferior to clerical works. This attitude is a handicap for fuller employment, economic growth and development in the Assamese society. We in Assam are still following the out dated approach to education. Even now the Arts Graduates dominate the field of education and most of them are not getting any job though their names are in the live registers of the employment exchanges for years together. This is to be checked and they should be informed of the scarcity of wage and paid jobs and also about the alternative facilities available for starting self-employment ventures.

The problem of unemployment in Assam has assumed such a magnitude that the planners have always stressed the need for arresting this wide spread problem through various planning process. But in spite of the best efforts the problem of unemployment could not be restrained yet. Whatever result could be achieved is neutralised by the factors like growth of population, rapid expansion of educational facilities and release of vast manpower in the Employment market.

Most of the educated job seekers of the state do not pass successfully in the examinations held by various Staff Selection Commission of the Central Government and other public sector undertakings. State Government may therefore provide necessary pre-recruitment training facilities to the local youths so that they could overcome their shortcomings and can compete with the candidates of advanced states.

According to the Seventh Plan document, the backlog of unemployment in India in March 1985 was the order of 9.20 million. However, during the period December 1984-July, 1989, the number of persons registered with the employment exchanges increased from 23.5 million to 31.6 million or by 34 per cent. The Seventh Plan was expected to generate about 40 million standard person years of employment. According to the E.M.I. programme employment in the organised sector of the economy increased by about one million during the first four years (upto December, 1988) of the Plan. Besides the special employment programme like NREP, IRDP, TRYSEM, two new employment programmes called the JAWAHAR ROZGAR YOZANA and NEHRU ROZGAR YOZANA have been introduced for the benefit of rural and urban unemployed persons respectively.*

---

* *Source*: (Agenda papers for 28th meeting of the Working Group on National Employment Service) held from 8th to 11th Nov. 1989.

The trend of unemployment in Assam was not much acute as it appears today. The reason for this also, are that economy of the State by then was mainly dependent on agricultural sector and the number of educated persons was also not very high in comparison to the available employment opportunities. The problem of unemployment assumed a serious proportion with the ever increasing expansion of educational institutions. In 1947-48 there were 7574 primary schools, 742 middle schools, 191 High Schools and 16 colleges. While in the year 1988-89 the position increased to 28,807 primary schools, 5,635 middle schools, 3,110 high and higher secondary schools and 181 colleges in the State.

The number of passed out candidates in the High/Higher Secondary examinations increased from 2,490 in 1947-48 to 69,008 in 1983-84 (*Source*: Directorate of Higher Secondary Education, Assam). The total number of educated job seekers registered with the employment exchanges was 1,44,800 in 1980 while it stood at 4,97,868 at the end of 1988. Thus the staggering growth of educated unemployed in Assam is also responsible for the acute unemployment problem in the State. Because the untrained educated do not match with the technical jobs.

There are short-comings both in the Employment Service as well as the Education Department. Before launching the new educational programme in the country we ought to have thought of appointing properly trained carreer masters in every school whose duty will be to maintain assessment cards of every students by which the guidance officers can assess the ability of a particular student in relation to his interest in particular course of study leading to particular field of occupation. Wrong choice of subject under the diversified carricular study leads not only to a frustrated person in his later vocational life but also cost the state exchequer to a great extent in making training facilities available in technical institutes and engineering colleges.

CHAPTER 2

Employment Service in Assam

The Constitution of India enjoins that the State shall take all steps within the limit of economic capacity and development for securing the right to work and to public assistance in case of unemployment.

Programmes of employment service are the joint responsibility of Central and State Governments. The employment service provides vocational guidance and placement of services to job seekers, assists employers with recruitment, collects and disseminates labour market information and conduct research into a variety of manpower problem. Besides, these functions, the service has also taken up schemes to provide self-employment assistance in many states. Substantial expansion has taken place in the network of the Employment Exchanges during the Seventh Plan. However, employment service has not yet extended to the State of Sikkim.

With a view to modernising operations at employment exchanges and providing efficient and objective services to the job seekers as well as to employers, the Central Govt. introduced from 1986-87 a centrally sponsored scheme on computerisation of employment exchanges as Seventh Plan Scheme.

The employment service in Assam was first set up in the mid-forties. After submission of the Shiva Rao Committee's report which was set up in 1952 the administration of the organisation was handed over to the State Govt. with effect from 1st November, 1956. By 1962 Employment Exchanges were set up in almost all the district head quarters and Sub-divisional towns.

In Assam at the end of the Sixth Five-Year Plan there were 47 employment exchanges (including three University Employment Information and Assistance Bureau with 26 Employment Market Information (EMI) units, 10 Vocational Guidance (V.G.) units and 20 Employment Information and Assistance Bureau.

During Seventh plan period employment service of the State expanded with the creation of 6 new employment exchanges and 9 E.I. & A. Bx. As such 53 employment exchanges including three universities employment & assistance bureaux and 33 E.I. & A. Bx have been functioning at the end of the Seventh Plan. The employment exchanges were also strengthened during the Seventh Plan by opening 13 units of District Manpower planning and Employment generation Councils, 7 E.M.I. units and 4 V.G. units.

During the Eighth Five-Year Plan it is proposed to set up 5 employment exchanges and 30 E.I. & A. Bx in the State. It is also proposed to strengthen 5 employment exchanges by setting up coaching cum guidance centres to give pre-examination coaching/training to the candidates applied for posts under various Public Sector recruiting agencies. During the Seventh Plan period, the District employment exchange, Guwahati has been brought under the computerisation scheme and the computer system have already been installed. During Eighth Plan period, it is proposed to computerise the employment exchange at Jorhat. The overall employment position of the State from 1984 to 1988 is as follows:

Statement Showing the Yearwise No. of Live Register, Registration Made, Applicants Submitted, Vacancies Notified to and Filled During the Five Year Period from 1984 to 1988 in the State of Assam

Description	At the end of Dec/84	At the end of Dec/85	At the end of Dec/86	At the end of Dec/87	At the end of Dec/88
1. No. of Live Register	4,89,848	5,96,055	8,15,251	8,54,415	9,03,702
2. Registration made during the year	1,94,704	1,58,214	2,23,655	1,68,191	1,66,797
3. Vacancies notified during the year	12,461	12,908	13,091	13,107	10,882
4. Applicants submitted during the year	1,10,042	1,11,094	1,54,174	1,45,936	1,04,556
5. Placement made during the year	6,484	6,279	5,241	5,538	6,347

Summary of the Important Statistics of Employment Exchanges in Assam as on 31st December, 1988

1. Number of Employment Exchanges	49
2. Number of U.E.I. & G. Bx	3
3. Number of E.E. & G. Bx	25
4. Number of applicants on Live Register	903702
(a) Ex-Servicemen	2566
(b) Scheduled Caste	45946
(c) Scheduled Tribe	81176
(d) Women	154358
(e) O.B.C.	233846
(f) Physically Handicapped	2966
5. Number of educated job seekers on Live Register	497868
(a) Engineering Graduate	1283
(b) Medical Graduate	244
(c) Agriculture	64
(d) Veterinary	—
(e) Passed out I.T.I. Trainees	13326
(f) Post-Graduate	3949
(g) Graduate	52963
(h) HSSLC/P.U./I.A. etc.	97905
(i) Matriculation/HSLC	324787
(j) Diplomaholders	3347

6. Number of applicants placed in employment during the year 1988	6347
(a) Ex-Servicemen	26
(b) Scheduled Caste	375
(c) Scheduled Tribe	519
(d) Women	540
(e) O.B.C.	829
(f) Physically Handicapped	23

Source: Directorate of Employment and Craftsmen Training, Assam.

The performance of Employment Exchanges during the year 1987 and 88 was as follows:

	Registration (000)	Vacancies notified (000)	Placement (000)	Applicants of (000)
1987	155.7	12.9	5.5	843.6
1988	160.1	10.6	6.4	903.8

Under the E.M.I. Programme the State covered 4834 Establishments under Public Sector and 1706 Establishments under Private Sector. The estimated employment at the end of March 31, 1989 in the State is as follows:

Public Sector

	Total	Women
i. Central Govt.	29007	3203
ii. State Govt.	257403	34027
iii. Central Qasi Govt.	70743	6140
iv. State Qasi Govt.	57913	9139
v. Local Bodies	11743	1607
Total	476809	54116

Private Sector

i. Large Establishments (25 & more)	509157	237679
ii. Smaller Establishments (10-24)	9432	738
Total	518589	238417

In addition the Employment Exchanges of the State under the Self-Employment Scheme also motivate and assist the self-employment seekers. The work done under this scheme upto June 1989 was as follows:

Sl. No.	Year	Registration Rural	Urban	Total	Beneficiaries
1.	1987	9402	6738	16140	1201
2.	1988	7844	4770	12614	623
3.	1989	4501	3683	3184	75

Upto June/89.

The employment exchanges also implement the "Unemployment Assistance Scheme, 1983" of this State. The number of beneficiaries and the amount distributed by the Employment Exchange under this scheme from 1983 to March, 1989 were 65,370 and Rs. 2,50,88,035.00 respectively.

In Assam a large number of registrants are there in the live registers of the employment exchanges. The exchanges have not been able to provide employment to them because many of the employers do not give necessary notification of the vacancies to the employment exchanges. Moreover candidates for Grade-III and Grade-IV posts are recruited through the employment exchanges only by the Govt. offices. The State Selection Commission, the Banking Service Selection Board do not give notification of their existing vacancies to the Employment Exchange for Grade-III services. They recruit independently. As such the State Selection

Commission, Banking Service Selection Board and the Railway Recruitment Board should be directed by the Govt. to give preference to the old registrants of the Employment Exchanges for appointment; subject to their qualifying in the test/interview and examination by the board.

The Data on employment and its occupational/educational pattern in the organised sector under the E.M.I. programme are collected by employment exchanges. The programme of vocational rehabilitation of handicapped persons has been expanded during the Seventh Plan. The network of coaching cum guidance centres for providing confidence building training and other employment guidance to work seekers also has been extended and presently the net work consists of 19 centres. Self-employment promotion cells are attached to the existing employment exchanges with a view to providing guidance to the job seekers and to motivate them for diversification to self-employment from salaried jobs. Vocational guidance and employment counselling units are functioning in 357 employment exchanges in the country.

In addition, University Employment Information and Guidance Bureaux are functioning at 81 universities in the country.

The units and the Bureaux assisted job seekers and the youths, in obtaining employment, occupational and educational information for planning their carriers. The need for providing guidance has increased due to launching at various employment and self-employment promotional programme for such areas. But the rate that the employment service can play in providing placement service to job seekers has been gradually reduced in scope, due to setting up of a number of commissions, Recruitment Boards etc. for sclection of personnel. This is supported by the fact that the number of vacancies being notified to the Employment Exchanges had been decreasing in the proceeding years. The number of vacancies notified to the Employment Exchanges remained around 8 to 9 lakhs for a fairly long time, but latter due to setting up of a number of commissions and recruitment boards, their number consistently decreased and during 1988 only 5.43 lakhs vacancies were notified. The number of job seekers registered with the employment exchanges, on the other hand been rapidly increasing. Thus the effectiveness of the placement function performed by the Employment Service has gone down and the Employment Exchanges are reduced to the status of an Agency merely for registering job seekers which is creating a demoralising effect on the job seekers. It is, therefore, necessary to take some steps to restore the rate of the employment services in providing placement services. It is necessary that the existing infrastructures of the employment exchange is utilised to the maximum extent for promotion of self-employment by giving it a more effective role in the self-employment programme. The role given by the Govt. at West Bengal, Kerala and Madhya Pradesh to employment exchange in assisting directly job seekers from live register into self-employment could perhaps be considered as a measure of policy.

One major problem facing by the job seekers registered in employment exchanges is that they do not get opportunity of any interview for several years till they become overaged. With the result the employment exchanges are becoming unpopular. Therefore to win the confidence of the job seekers and to make the employment service more useful, the procedure of submission of candidates who are likely to be overaged without strictly adhering to seniority norms should be adopted. Three years old registration may be insisted for claiming this benefit.

During December, 1984 to July 1989 the number of registered job seekers alone increased from 23.5 million to 31.6 million i.e. by 34 per cent. The 1st Five-Year Plan began with a live register figure of only 3.29 lakhs of unemployed persons registered with employment exchanges. The figures gradually rose to 18.35 lakhs in 1961, 51 lakhs in 1971 and 165.54 lakhs in 1981.

It was believed that various measures taken for economic development of the country will generate adequate employment for our growing population. This hope has been belied and the problem of unemployment has grown more acute. Placement in jobs through employment exchanges has been gradually declining. Only one out of 100 registered job seekers is annually placed in a job. Further the number of unemployed persons registered with employment exchanges is a fraction of the total number of the unemployed and underemployed persons in our country. Assuming an annual growth rate of 2.5 per cent per annum since the last Census of 1981, the total population of India may be estimated at 822.70 million in 1989. 44.3 per cent of this population i.e. 361.70 million constitute the effective employable workforce of India. As against this the organised sector of the economy is estimated to have employed only 25.93 million persons as on 30.6.88 which stood at 25.06 million persons in 1986. This is a matter of serious concern to the policy makers of the country, since no nation can afford wastage of this manpower resources. Therefore, the question of chosing a socially appropriate technology which will open scope for more employment is of prime importance.

Programme of employment service are the joint responsibility of the Central and State Govt. Development and administration of the programme at the National level are looked after by the Directorate General of Employment and Training, while the responsibility for the day to day Administration of employment Exchanges rests with the State Governments and Union Territory Administration. In Assam the employment exchanges are doing the old traditional functions only, except payment of unemployment allowance to the educated unemployed. This scheme has been started very recently. With the realisation that wage paid job cannot be provided to all the job seekers. There has been a greater stress on promotion of self-employment. Some of the States like Kerala, Madhya Pradesh, West Bengal are undertaking activities in this regard by not only guiding and motivating job seekers but also providing some kind of self-employment assistance. On an average throughout India the employment exchanges register about 60 lakhs job seekers in a year.

Number of vacancies notified to and placements made by the employment exchanges have declined substantially in recent years and in the year 1987/88/89, it stands around 5 to 6 lakhs, and 3 to 4 lakhs in a year registerables goes out of employment. They remain as burden of their parents.

Annexure 1 on the following pages, gives the State-wise numbers of Employment Exchanges and other salient statistical information connected with their activities.

The employment situation in Assam remained more or less static during the past few years. At present, there are 53 Employment Exchanges including 3 (three) University Employment Information and Assistance Bureaux are functioning in the State. The performance of the Employment Exchanges during the 1988 and 1989 was as follows:

Registration	Vacancies notified	Placement	Applicants on live register at the end of the year (in thousand)
1987—155.7	12.9	5.5	843.6
1988—160.1	10.6	6.4	903.8

Source: Directorate of Employment, Assam.

Annexure 1

Performance of Employment Exchanges—Statewise 1988

Sl. No.	States/Union Territories	Employment Exchanges/ UEIGBX (at end of year)	In thousands				
			Registra-tions	Vacancies notified	Submission	Placements	Application live register (at end of year)
	States						
1.	Andhra Pradesh	33	397.0	41.7	340.7	19.5	2676.1
2.	Arunachal Pradesh	1	0.6	0.1	—	—	4.6
3.	Assam	52	160.1	10.6	104.7	6.4	903.8
4.	Bihar	63	508.2	19.7	283.3	18.7	2657.6
5.	Goa	1	16.1	1.9	43.4	1.9	74.3
6.	Gujarat	42	184.8	30.3	188.6	13.0	863.3
7.	Haryana	87	243.4	33.1	189.3	12.1	577.1
8.	Himachal Pradesh	15	80.3	8.7	195.9	7.1	367.8
9.	Jammu & Kashmir	14	30.2	3.6	34.7	1.5	129.8
10.	Karnataka	37	205.8	17.0	171.6	8.4	1058.2
11.	Kerala	40	344.7	22.9	178.8	15.6	2901.1
12.	Madhya Pradesh	63	508.5	34.7	207.8	25.3	1788.2
13.	Maharashtra	43	555.7	52.8	496.4	29.7	2663.7
14.	Manipur	9	24.9	2.9	21.9	0.4	245.5

15.	Meghalaya	7	6.1	0.7	4.3	0.3	20.7
16.	Mizoram	3	9.0	3.4	33.2	1.5	38.5
17.	Nagaland	7	8.1	2.6	10.7	0.5	25.0
18.	Orissa	24	162.3	20.8	211.0	0.0	745.0
19.	Punjab	40	196.7	22.7	198.2	9.0	576.1
20.	Rajasthan	31	203.3	23.6	237.7	13.3	850.8
21.	Sikkim*	—	—	—	—	—	—
22.	Tamil Nadu	33	512.3	67.0	891.9	50.6	2607.6
23.	Tripura	4	34	3.6	35.7	1.7	135.6
24.	Uttar Pradesh	94	846.0	43.7	362.0	29.1	2974.5
25.	West Bengal	69	499.6	22.3	181.3	12.9	4188.8
	Union Territories						
1.	Andaman and Nicobar	1	5.2	2.0	21.3	1.4	15.1
2.	Chandigarh	2	31.0	3.5	35.4	1.4	142.7
3.	Dadra and Nagar Haveli	1	0.4	0.2	2.8	0.1	1.8
4.	Daman and Diu**	2	—	—	—	—	—
5.	Delhi	20	175.1	34.5	180.8	36.0	706.4
6.	Lakshadweep	1	0.9	—	1.6	@	7.8
7.	Pondicherry	1	12.5	4.0	42.5	1.4	102.8
				6.4			
All India : Total		840	5963.2	543.3	4907.4	328.5	30050.2

Note: 1. * No employment exchange is functioning. 2. ** Data are not maintained.3. Figure less than 50. @.
4. Figures may not add up to total, due to rounding off.

Over and above the Registration/Placement/Submission etc. the employment exchanges also implement the unemployment Assistance Scheme 1983 of Assam. Total amount disbursed under the scheme from 1983 to March 1989 was Rs. 2,50,88,035.00 and the total number of beneficiaries benefited is 65,370.

During the Seventh Plan period, the District Employment Exchange, Guwahati has been brought under the computerisation scheme. During Eighth Plan period, it is proposed to computerise the employment exchange at Jorhat.

Registration of job seekers and sponsoring them for placement against vacancies notified by the employers is most important activity performed by the employment exchanges.

The employment exchange (compulsory notification of vacancies Act, 1959) required all public sector establishments and such non-agricultural establishments in this private sector with 25 or more workers to compulsorily notify their vacancies, other than those filled through Public Service Commission and similar agencies and other exempted under the Act to the local employment exchanges. The number of vacancies received by the Employment Exchanges have remained more or less steady around 8 to 9 lakhs per year for a long time till 1983 without any increasing trend. It will be clear from the enclosed Annexure 2 that in recent years there has been a steady decline in the vacancies notified to the employment exchanges and in the number of placement also made by the exchanges.

Annexure 2

Number of Registrations, Vacancies Notified, Placements and the Number of Job Seekers on the Live Register (1980-88)

Year	No. of employment exchanges at end of the year	In thousands				
		Registrations	Vacancies notified	Placements	Live register at the end of year	Percentage increased in live register over the previous year
1980	638	6158.2	837.7	477.7	16200.3	13.0
1981	663	6276.9	896.8	504.1	17838.1	10.1
1982	692	5862.9	819.9	473.4	19753.0	10.7
1983	726	6755.8	826.0	485.9	21953.3	11.1
1984	745	6219.0	707.8	407.3	23546.8	7.3
1985	800	5821.5	674.7	388.5	26269.9	11.6
1986	821	5535.4	623.4	351.3	30131.2	14.7
1987	835	6011.7	600.9	334.4	30247.3	0.4
1988	840	5963.2	543.3	328.5	30050.2	– 0.7

Source: Report of the Working Group on Employment Service, 1989.

While the private sector industries/establishments have hardly utilised the employment exchanges for their recruitment, the number of public sector recruitment agencies such as Banking Recruitment Board, the Staff Selection Commission etc. have also increased. The role of the employment exchange as a placement agency has become gradually unimportant.

On the other hand the job seekers continue to consider the employment exchanges as an important means to secure employment. The number of persons on the live registers of the employment exchanges is swelling year by year. On an average about 60 lakhs new registrants are added to the total number of job keepers is over 300 lakhs against an annual demand of 6 lakhs. But the live registers of the employment exchanges do not show the actual data of unemployment because of the following reasons:

1. Registration with an employment exchange is voluntary. All unemployed may not register with the employment exchanges.
2. Most of the employment exchanges are located in urban areas and as such most of the unemployed and underemployed in the rural sector do not find it convenient to register themselves.

Persons already in employment may also have registered in search of better job opportunities. For the above reasons the data available with the employment exchanges do not serve as real indicators of unemployment in the State. If the data of the employment exchanges are taken as the parameter of the trend of unemployment in the State, it is found that total number of registrants seeking jobs are increasing at a fast rate from year to year. The total number of job seekers in May, 1981 was 3,60,343. It rose to 8,32,426 in May, 1987. The educational level of the unemployed (50 per cent were matriculates or above.)

But only 3.5 per cent of the registrants get a chance of placement every year. In Assam the high level of unemployment is due to two main factors:

(a) High growth of population

(b) Low growth of economy.

These two sets of factors have been operating in both the urban and rural sector. Due to inflow of people from the rural areas. The urban population is increasing daily.

The bulk of the State populations (89.4 per cent) projected for 1981 live in the rural sector. But the agricultural activities has been more or less stagnant, non-agricultural activity also have not expanded, resultantly the stagnant rural income has to maintain an increasing labour force giving rise to large-scale employment and unemployment.

In the urban areas the stagnant growth of economic activities have failed to generate employment opportunities for the skilled/semi-skilled and unskilled people coming from the rural areas.

The slow growth of economic development have so far failed to generate employment for the educated people. The result has been an ever increase in the field of unemployment both in the educated and uneducated sector which is leading to a labour surplus economy.

There is the need to vocationalisation of education and diversification of trades and courses under the new education policy whose main purpose should be to increase individual employability, by reducing mismatch between the demand and supply of skilled manpower and also to provide alternative for those pursuing aimless higher education. State should therefore provide vocational guidance services to the student community.

The entire labour force cannot be provided with wagepaid employment therefore the unemployed youths should be diverted to take up self-employment as an alternative to wage paid job.

Impact is to be created for awareness amongst the unemployed to take up self-employment as an alternative to wage paid job.

Assam and North-Eastern States comprising of Meghalaya, Manipur, Nagaland, Mizoram, Tripura and Arunachal Pradesh are significantly backward in terms of industrialisation, while Assam has few industries and the net domestic product of the manufacturing sector during 1981 was of Rs. 408 crores, other states have hardly any industries. Though the first commercial exploitation of crude oil took place in Assam, further development had been quite tardy. The entire region had a total population of 261 lakhs during 1981 spread over a geographical area of 233 thousand sq km. All the North-Eastern States are economically underdeveloped. The region is predominantly agriculture based with forest and natural resources. It also accounts for bulk of the country's Tea production. The major industrial and commercial centres in the region are Guwahati, Tinsukia, Silchar, Dibrugarh and Shillong.

As per the data available in the employment exchanges in Assam, the total number of unemployed in the live register as on 31-12-89 is 9,77,126 as against 3,73,035 in 1981 i.e. during last seven years the number of unemployed increased in Assam to more than double. The picture of the unemployed in the year 1988 as per the live register of the employment exchanges is given below:

Number of Applicants on the Live Register as on 31-12-89

1. Total no. on Live Register	—	977126
2. Total no. of Educated Applicants	—	552215
3. Matriculate/HSLC passed	—	351305
4. HSSLC/P.U./I.A.	—	117333
5. Graduate	—	61018
6. Post-Graduates	—	4088
7. Pass out I.T.I.		
(a) Engineering trade	—	12622
(b) Non-Engineering trade	—	1227
8. Agricultural Graduates	—	120
9. Medical Graduates	—	254
10. Engineering Graduates	—	1416

This explosive situation of unemployment is creating frustration amongst the coming generation, which is leading the entire State into social tension.

CHAPTER 3

Employment Service in South-East Asia

India has the best organised employment service in the Asian Region. It has well established institutional arrangement with the working group on the national employment service at the apex level and similar advisory bodies down to district level. The growth of the employment service from about 70 exchanges at the time of independence to about 900 employment exchanges in 40 years is quite significant. The employment service in Bangladesh has been reorganised; with direct responsibilities for overseas employment, self-employment, labour market information, vocational guidance and local employment service. Bangladesh employment service has taken up self-employment promotion in rural as well as urban areas through credit and micro enterprise schemes. In Bangladesh the countries exchequer is heavily dependent on remittances from wage earners abroad to meet foreign exchange requirement. More than one lakh workers from Bangladesh are there in Iraq and Kuwait and they are sending 100 million U.S. dollars. According to official estimates annual remittance from wage earners abroad are estimated at 800 million U.S. dollars. Fresh efforts are being made for finding employment opportunity in the far eastern countries particularly in Japan, South Korea, Hongkong, Malasiya and Singapore. Bangladesh Association of International Recruiting Agencies (BAIRA) and Bangladesh Overseas Employment Service (BOESL) are exploring job opportunity for Bangladeshies in foreign countries.

In Thailand, the Employment Service Division of the labour department together with 18 employment service offices in Bangkok and a small unit in each of the provincial offices constitute the national service. Each of the field officer is supplied with a comprehensive data base on establishment in their respective jurisdiction which facilitates canvassing vacancies and contacts with managements. Vacancies notified to individual offices are pooled on the computer at the end of each day in the head office and a comperhensive list is displayed in all the offices in Bangkok next day and in regional offices on the next day.

Job seekers who apply against suitable vacancy are interviewed and referred to employers. *JOB BAZARS* are organised in provincial educational centres which provide an opportunity to job seekers and employers to meet and exchange information. Each job bazar places an average 10,000 job seekers in employment.

The Indonesian Employment Service comprises of the Directoratc General of Manpower Supply and Placement in the Department of Manpower in Jakarta, and an employment exchange in about 180 district manpower offices. Job seekers are interviewed at the time of registration and are given advice on job prospects and then referred to employers against vacancies displayed. In addition, there is a sub-directorate called *BINAPAKSI* with responsibilities to promote self-employment. A self-employment promoter of *BINAPAKSI* is posted in selected district manpower offices to help persons interested in self-employment with information and assistance.

In Sri Lanka, the employment services were abolished several years ago and local offices of the department of labour are being involved in self-employment promotion.

In Nepal also employment service functions are not yet organised and labour supply centres are the only units that serves as employment centres. In China employment services are in the process of establishment. In China currently, labour services company perform employment promotion activities. Hongkong has also a well-organised employment service.

To evaluate the performance of the employment service, we are to seek answers, whether the demand for registration in the employment offices, among the unemployed and the demand for manpower from the employers have shown any variation over a period of time say during previous five years. There has been a gradual decline in registrations from 6.75 million to 6.01 million between 1983-87, though there was an increase in the number of employment exchanges during the same period from 619 to 755. This indicates that the labour force which is increasing at a rate of 2.6 per cent per year are looking elsewhere for employment assistance. For them the employment exchanges are no longer the dependable agencies to secure early employment. The demand for manpower has fallen more than that for registration during the same period. Vacancies notified to the employment exchanges in India declined from 0.8 million in 1983 to 0.6 million in 1987.

As for the labour market information, Indian employment service is a good model in South-East Asia. But the E.M.I. data suffer from many serious limitations, inadequate coverage and delay in processing. The scope of using the data for labour department programmes such as craftsmen and apprenticeship training programmes, vocational guidance etc. has remained unexploited. The manner of presentation of the data is very important. The situation therefore warrants the need for non-traditional approaches. In a labour surplus situation, utility of employment exchanges based on traditional approach will always be questioned. A serious review of the employment service is necessary to identify appropriate re-orientation to its role and functions specially.

In the context of development strategies in India unemployment problem is so deeprooted that the employment services cannot be expected to perform as efficiently as in developed countries. The main role of the employment service should be to remove the deficiencies in the smooth operation of the labour market.

Economic growth alone cannot create enough employment. Long-term unemployment is socially and economically dangerous phenomenon. Modernisation of enterprises is immediately necessary to solve this problem.

A variety of job creation programmes, classified as L.E.I.'s (local employment initiative) has been introduced in most of the Western countries. In U.K. alone these programmes cost annually more than two billion British pounds. The L.E.I's principal role played by local level institutions in the job creation programme with financial and other subsidies from the central office of the Employment Service.

The Filipino Employment Service Network, like in Indonesia, is not independent of Labour Department Network. At the regional level the fourteen Regional Offices of the Department of Labour and Employment (DOLE) have one Employment Promotion Division, each of which is responsible for delivery of the placement services under the direct supervision of Regional Director. The DOLE is presently promoting establishment of full-time or part-time community employment centres at the grass-root level as part of the local administrations from their own resources. Within the Department of Labour and Employment, the Bureau of Local Employment (B.L.E.) functions as the Headquarters of the Employment Service and it concerns itself with policies and procedures and training of personnel. Labour market information is collected through the network of DOLE provincial/district offices. Recently B.L.E. has been assigned the responsibility of coordinating the self-employment programmes of the various Bureaux of DOLE and is also assisting them with information packaging. Within DOLE, Bureau of Rural Workers, Bureau of Young and Minor Workers, NMYC, and Bureau of Labour Relations undertake what is known in Philippines as Livelihood Programmes. The important feature in Malaysia is the linkage with Board of Investment for meeting the manpower requirement of new investments. Bangladesh, Philippines and Indonesia are currently implementing an ILO/DANIDA Project on promoting self-employment.

In Nepal, it was revealed in a similar analysis that most of the job information (76 per cent) to beneficiaries of Labour Supply Centres, came through informal channels (Naike). Special programmes for procurement of information on vacancies have been noticed in Hong Kong and Indonesia. Thailand Employment Service disseminates information on newspaper vacancies and refers applicants against the newspaper vacancies. The location of Bangkok city employment exchanges are in railway stations, bus stations and similar other places mainly to cater to the rural migrants. In Hong Kong, regular advertisements appear on TV advocating use of employment services by the employers. In general, the emphasis seems to be more on dissemination of vacancy information than on registration. Employers' reasons for non-use of employment service, as seen in annual reviews in Malaysia include: low-quality of applicants, restricted choice, and lack of expertise in interviewing applicants. These factors make it necessary to induce local offices to adopt innovative approaches.

We have no data on vocational guidance programme to make objective assessment of its performances. The vocational guidance services have proved relatively more effective in smaller countries in South Pacific or in cases where shortages have emerged. One reason for this is joint programmes with Ministry of Education. In Solomon Island and in Hong Kong, the employment service trains the vocational teachers of schools and in Thailand, Hong Kong, Singapore mass media is used for vocational guidance. However, in majority of countries, participation in guidance activities is reported to be insignificant. The reason seems to be lack of knowledge on 'vocations' to which the young persons can be guided.

As for the labour market information, Indian Employment Service was a good model in this region some years ago. It is well known that the E.M.I. data suffer from many serious limitations including inadequate coverage and delay in processing. Reports that are brought out at various levels year after year meticulously, are hardly used. The scope of using the data for labour Ministry's programmes such as the craftsmen and apprenticeship training programmes, wage determination, vocational guidance and investment promotion has remained unexploited. The manner of presentation of data is extremely important. Australia has started producing different sets of labour market information reports for specific policies such as wages, job creation, industrial relations and working conditions.

To sum up the review, the situation seems to suggest the need for adoption of non-traditional and innovative approaches. In a labour surplus situation, utility of employment exchanges based on traditional approaches, will always be questioned as has been the case in Bangladesh recently. A few years ago a High Court judgment nearly paralysed the employment service in an Indian State and fortunately a subsequent Supreme Court judgment restored the status quo. An I.L.O. mission to Sri Lanka in the late sixties raised the same question. In some countries in Africa, traditional approach with legal backing has not produced the desired result.

An important reason for attrition of employment service in most countries can be found in its gradual isolation over the past decades from the mainstream of national development. The service remained blind and insensitive to the development needs of the community.

In Japan, an Employment Service is considered a basic service, like that of a school, hospital, post office or railway station. Ideally, it should be so. In Japan, there is no structural unemployment and employment services are more effective in dealing with what is known as *Frictional Unemployment.* In developing countries, the employment problem is deep-rooted in the structure of the economy and it will be unrealistic to expect the employment services to perform as efficiently as in developed countries.

What is however surprising, is that no conscious policy has been adopted in most developing Asian countries to influence job-creation through specific agencies such as Employment Service. The developing economies, for several decades now, are advocating employment promotion/poverty alleviation measures through programmes such as IRDP, Livelihood Programme, and other Development Programmes. From the findings of an ARPLA Project covering Bangladesh, Indonesia and Philippines, it has become evident that the size of these programmes are far too inadequate to bring any change in the structure in several decades to come. There is no agency to monitor the employment impact of investments made, be that in the modern sector or traditional sector. Employment lost due to use of agricultural land for urbanisation, housing, industrial development and other purposes is never taken into account. Employment lost or delayed due to unutilised manufacturing capacity, bureaucratic red tape, trade union pressure or employers bias or irrational job-preference of job seekers not to speak of proliferation of institutions turning out unemployable youths do not seem to cause concern among the policy-makers. Nor the employment service have attempted to present these situations to the policy-makers. In reality there is no forum where we could present them nor are we really prepared to service such forums if they were to come into existence. The main role of the employment service should be to remove the deficiencies and bottlenecks in the smooth operation of the labour market. *Efficiency and Equity* in the labour market is the ultimate goal for which employment services should operate. In developing economies, efficiency of the economy suffers largely because of wrong selection, inappropriate recruitment practices, and limited dissemination of information on job-opportunities—be that wage job or self-employment. Many of the developmental facilities, including credit, training, industrial or agricultural extension services technology centres remain underutilised and largely inaccessible to those for whom these services are meant. 'Excess liquidity' characterises the banking system in many countries because of limited concept of 'creditworthy' activities, causing adverse employment impact. The educational institutions do not train persons for preparation of credit-worthy activities. The vacuum exists and there is no reason why employment service cannot step in.

We have borrowed the concept of employment service from the West. We have not however followed the changes that have occurred in these services. In recent years, the unemployment situation in these countries has worsened as may be seen from the following table:

Percentage of Unemployed in EC Countries 1987

Belgium	— 13.4	Italy	— 12.8
Denmark	— 7.7	Luxembourg	— 1.2
France	— 10.7	Netherlands	— 11.1
FRG	— 7.7	Portugal	— 8.5
Greece	— 8.3	Spain	— 21.5
Irish Republic	— 18.0	UK	— 12.0

Source: ARPLA Database Social and Labour Bulletin 2/89.

These rates of unemployment, except in case of Luxembourg, have exceeded the limits of 'Frictional Unemployment'. Structural adjustments are being sought in these countries, simultaneously, with what is known as job-creation programmes through the employment services. These policies of job-creation are based on the realisation that:

(a) economic growth alone cannot create enough employment;

(b) modernisation of enterprises is essential and

(c) long-term unemployment is a socially and economically unacceptable phenomenon.

A variety of job-creation programmes, now classified as L.E.I.'s (Local Employment Initiative) has been introduced in most of these countries. In UK, alone these programmes cost annually more than two billion British

Pounds. The name LEI, is due to the principal role played by local level institutions in the job-creation programmes with financial and other subsidies from the Central Office of the Employment Service. On December 1, 1988, France has adopted a legislation on 'Minimum Integration Income' for persons including 0.4 million long-term unemployed. This is in addition to the LEI programmes such as training, retraining, subsidy to employers, local institutions and others for job-creation, special programmes for depressed regions. While isolated programmes of job-creation of these varieties exist in India and several other Asian countries, the employment services have remained away from these types of activities. The magnitude of the problem in developing countries is so large that much more needs to be done and given a proper mechanism of coordination, by many more agencies.

The employment service should establish linkage with the communities at the village level. Each Gram Panchayat should be converted into a community employment service and the State/National Employment Service should train them in adopting programmes to mitigate seasonal unemployment generating confidence among the rural unemployed youth in their own employability. These community employment services should be a source of information on self-employment opportunities and facilities in their respective areas. The wage-paid jobs in our country are limited and the job opportunities do not keep pace with ever-increasing number of job seekers. It is therefore necessary that the area of self-employment is explored.

CHAPTER 4

Employment Situation and Employment Service in India and Assam

EMPLOYMENT SCENE

According to the Seventh Plan Document, the backlog of unemployment in March, 1985 was of the order of 9.20 million in the age-group 5+. The information of unemployment for subsequent years in not available.

However, during the period December 1984-July 1989, the number of persons registered with the Employment Exchanges increased from 23.5 million to 31.6 million or by 34 per cent. For obvious reasons, the Employment Exchange statistics do not provide a true index of unemployment situation. However, the recent survey conducted by the DGE&T to ascertain the proportion of employed persons among the Employment Exchange registrants, the results of which are being finalised, would help in correcting the Employment Exchange statistics as an indicator of unemployment to some extent.

The Seventh Plan expected to generate about 40 million Standard Person Years of Employment. Information on employment so far generated during the Plan is not available. However, according to the EMI Programme, employment in the organised sector of the economy increased by about one million during the first four years (upto December, 1988) of the Plan. The special employment programmes like NREP, RLEGP, Self-Employment Programme for Educated Unemployed Youth and for Urban Poor, etc. have, however, been generating employment by and large as per expectations.

During the current year, two new employment programmes called the *Jawahar Rozgar Yojana* and *Nehru Rozgar Yojana* have been introduced for the benefit of rural and urban unemployed persons respectively. The National Rural Employment Programme (NREP) and the Rural Landless Employment Guarantee Programme (RLEGP) have been merged with Jawahar Rozgar Yojana. 80 per cent of the funds for Jawahar Rozgar

Yojana and Nehru Rozgar Yojana would be provided by the Central Government.

The State Governments have also been implementing special employment programmes like Maharashtra Employment Guarantee Scheme, Land Army Scheme of Karnataka, Self-Employment Scheme of West Bengal and Kerala, etc.

PERFORMANCE OF EMPLOYMENT EXCHANGES

Registration of job seekers and their placement against vacancies notified by the employers is one of the main activities of the Employment Exchanges. The number of Employment Exchanges in the country has increased from 745 at the beginning of 1985 to 840 at the beginning of 1989, thereby providing facilities of the Employment Exchanges to a number of small towns. The Live Register of Employment Exchanges marginally declined from 302.4 lakhs at the end of 1987 to 300.5 lakhs at the end of 1988. The number of vacancies notified to the Employment Exchanges have also gone down from 6.0 lakhs in 1987 to 5.4 lakhs in 1988, continuing the trend observed since 1983. The placements through the National Employment Service have also declined from 3.34 lakhs to 3.28 lakhs during the same period. The registrations effected by the Employment Exchanges during this period have remained the same (60 lakhs) in both the years. Statement showing the performance of the Employment Exchanges during the last 9 years is enclosed (Statement 1).

Statement 1

Performance of Employment Exchanges—All India 1980-1988

Year	Employment Exchanges/ UEIGEx (at end of year)	In thousands						
		Registrations	Placements	Percentage of placements to registrations	Vacancies notified	Percentage of placements to vacancies notified	Live register	Percentage increase in live register over previous year
1980	638	6158.2	477.7	7.8	837.7	57.0	16200.3	13.0
1981	663	6276.9	504.1	8.0	896.8	56.2	17838.1	10.1
1982	692	5862.9	473.4	8.1	819.9	57.7	19753.0	10.7
1983	726	6755.8	485.9	7.2	826.0	58.8	21953.3	11.1
1984	745	6219.0	407.3	6.5	707.8	57.5	23546.8	7.3
1985	800	5821.5	388.5	6.7	674.7	57.6	26269.9	11.6
1986	821	5535.4	351.3	6.3	623.4	56.4	30131.2	14.7
1987	835	6011.7	334.4	5.6	600.9	55.7	30247.3	0.4
1988	840	5963.2	328.5	5.5	543.3	60.5	30050.2	0.7

Source: Agenda papers, 28th Meeting of the Working Group on National Employment Service-I.

The comparative performance of Employment Exchanges and UEIGBx in the States/UTs during the years 1987 and 1988 has been given in Statement 2. It may be observed that the registrations in the States of A.P., Gujarat, Haryana, H.P., J & K, Manipur, Mizoram, Orissa, Punjab, Rajasthan, Tamil Nadu, have shown a declining trend during 1988 as compared with the year 1987. The number of vacancies notified to the Employment Exchanges in the States have also gone down in most of the States during 1988 as compared to the previous year. Increasing trend has been observed in the field of placement in the States of Assam, Goa, Kerala, M.P., Mizoram, Tamil Nadu, West Bengal, etc. The live registers, has shown an increasing trend in the States of Assam, H.P., J & K, Karnataka, M.P., Maharashtra, Mizoram, Rajasthan, Tamil Nadu, Tripura and U.P. etc.

14.	Manipur	29.7	24.9	5.4	2.9	0.8	0.4	286.8	245.5
15.	Meghalaya	6.9	6.1	0.8	0.7	0.2	0.3	19.1	20.7
16.	Mizoram	17.0	9.0	2.3	3.4	1.0	1.5	37.4	38.5
17.	Nagaland	4.6	8.1	1.2	2.0	0.4	0.5	23.2	25.0
18.	Orissa	191.8	162.3	20.2	20.8	11.2	10.0	791.9	745.0
19.	Punjab	213.7	196.7	25.1	22.7	9.4	9.0	619.0	576.1
20.	Rajasthan	232.3	203.3	26.2	23.6	16.6	13.3	831.2	850.8
21.	Sikkim	—	—	—	—	—	—	—	—
22.	Tamil Nadu	540.3	512.3	63.0	67.0	45.6	50.6	2486.2	2607.6
23.	Tripura	14.6	34.5	1.8	3.6	2.0	1.7	117.5	135.6
24.	Uttar Pradesh	749.4	846.0	46.9	43.7	28.0	29.1	2963.4	2974.5
25.	West Bengal	454.1	499.6	25.4	22.8	10.1	12.9	4564.7	4188.8
	Union Territories								
1.	Andaman and Nicobar Islands	4.4	5.2	1.8	2.0	1.0	.4	16.0	15.1
2.	Chandigarh	28.2	31.6	3.3	3.5	1.8	.4	137.2	142.7
3.	Dadra and Nagar Haveli**	—	0.4	—	0.2	—	0.1	—	1.8
4.	Daman and Diu**	—	—	—	—	—	—	—	—
5.	Delhi	182.0	175.1	31.4	34.5	45.5	36.0	706.3	706.4
6.	Lakshadweep	—	0.9	—	—	—	—	—	7.8
7.	Pondicherry Central Employment Exchange	9.7	12.5	1.9	4.0	0.3	.4	91.6	102.8
			4.3	6.4					
	All India Total	6011.7	5963.2	600.9	543.3	334.4	328.5	30247.3	30050.2

Source: Agenda paper, 28th Meeting of the Working Group on National Employment Service.

Statement 2

Performance of Employment Exchanges and University Employment Information and Guidance Bureaux in Different States/Union Territory during 1987 and 1988

Sl. No.	States/Union territories	No. of registrations effected during Jan.-Dec.		No. of vacancies notified during Jan.-Dec.		No. of placements affected during Jan.-Dec.		No. of applicants on the live register at the end of Dec.	
		1987	1988	1987	1988	1987	1988	1987	1988
	States								
1.	Andhra Pradesh	451.6	397.0	55.7	41.7	20.6	19.5	2722.0	2676.1
2.	Arunachal Pradesh	—	0.6	—	0.1	—	—	—	4.6
3.	Assam	155.7	160.1	12.9	10.6	5.5	6.4	843.6	903.8
4.	Bihar	496.5	508.2	28.5	19.7	20.5	18.7	2708.1	2657.6
5.	Goa	13.1	16.1	4.6	3.9	1.1	1.9	78.2	74.3
6.	Gujarat	197.7	184.8	34.4	30.3	13.7	13.0	781.8	363.3
7.	Haryana	281.0	243.4	33.8	33.1	13.8	12.1	579.8	577.1
8.	Jammu & Kashmir	38.8	30.2	3.4	3.6	2.3	1.5	127.4	129.8
9.	Himachal Pradesh	82.0	80.3	25.5	8.7	7.6	7.1	349.7	367.8
10.	Karnataka	214.9	205.8	21.4	17.0	8.8	8.4	1012.6	1058.2
11.	Kerala	442.9	344.7	24.1	22.9	14.1	15.6	2990.1	2901.1
12.	Madhya Pradesh	415.3	508.5	34.6	34.7	23.1	25.3	1748.3	1788.2
13.	Maharashtra	543.3	555.7	61.0	52.8	30.3	29.7	2615.4	2663.7

(Contd.)

CHAPTER 5

Manpower Information

In Assam the manpower information from the organised sector is collected under the employment market information programme. In Assam there are 52 employment exchanges out of which 34 employment exchanges have E.M.I. unit including all the 23 district employment exchanges. Till March, 1989, 6540 establishments have been covered under this programme. Sector wise break up of establishment are as follows:

Public Sector	:	4834
Private Sector	:	1706
Total		6540

Due to the following reasons the employment exchanges are not in a position to achieve good response from the employers. The major problem for which the employment exchanges face difficulty in collecting manpower data from the establishments. Is lacuna in the Employment Exchanges (C.N.V.) Act, 1959. The punishment for non-furnishing of manpower information by the employers is very negligible. It should be made cognigible and the penalty should be simple imprisonment with fine. The employment exchanges are experiencing difficulty in collection of data from public sector establishments. The employers in public sector are to some extent reluctant to comply with the request made by employment exchanges for submission of returns. Government therefore, over and above the legal provisions in the Act should take appropriate action against defaulting government and public sector employers. People should establish a fact and compromise between their potential and occupational opportunities available in the employment market. There are approximately forty thousand occupations in the developed countries, because of advanced technology. There are varieties of occupations, but in the developing countries where there are not so many sophisticated occupations, the numbers of occupations are less than those in developed countries. As per national directory of classification of occupation there are about 2500 occupations in India.

The question therefore arises as to whether unemployment in Assam is increasing due to non-availability of skilled manpower or due to lack of employability of the available manpower. Employment generated in the organised sector during five year plan period i.e., from

1984 to 1989 is increasing @ 2.5 per cent annually. On the basis of the information provided by I.A.M.R. working group on manpower development and from the information available from the live registers of the employment exchanges, the positions of demand and supply of the educated manpower in Assam during 8th and 9th plan period is shown below:

Demand and Supply Position of Educated Manpower Requirement during 8th and 9th Plan Period in Assam

Education level		8th plan balance		9th plan balance
A. Graduate and above				
1. Graduate and above in Arts/Science/Commerce and other general subjects	+	79,797		1,12,515
2. Graduate and above in Education (PG)	+	3,720		6,303
3. Graduate and above in Agriculture	–	836	–	1,388
4. Graduate and above in Veterinary Science	–	672	–	854
5. Graduate and above in Medicine	–	1,026	–	1,832
6. Graduate and above in Engineering Technology	–	3,125	–	4,799

Contd.

7. Graduate and above in other technical field/ professional/CA/ Company Secretaries	–	3,936	–	6,682
B. Below Graduate but above Matric				
8. Diploma in Agriculture	–	9	–	10
9. Diploma in Veterinary Science	–	118	–	243
10. Diploma in Engg./Tech.	–	657	–	174
11. Diploma in Midwifery and Nursing	–	145	–	154
12. Other Diploma	–	221	–	342
13. ITI Certificates	+	15,776	+	22,355
14. Certificate in Education	–	17,064	–	16,647
15. Matric & above but below Graduate (General)	+	7,30,898	+	10,00,163
16. Other Certificates	–	2,524	–	3,403
Total	+	7,99,858	+	11,04,808

(+) Excess Supply

(–) Short Supply

Source: *Assam Tribune*, dated 27.8.90.

It is therefore apparent that by the end of Eighth Five-Year Plan 7.99 lakhs educated job seekers will remain unemployed and by the end of 9th Plan period

11.04 lakhs.

There is shortage of technical and professionals, during the Eighth Plan period; this shortage will assume various dimensions. The state therefore should take up schemes immediately to develop experienced manpower. The unemployed technical manpower of the state should be placed under apprenticeship training with the undertakings in their specialised areas throughout the country, so that their employability is enhanced and they make themselves fit for appointment in the Noomaligarh Refinery, the Gas Cracker project including the other identified and already existing projects.

In the General disciplines, the facilities at the graduate level colleges may be modified instead of giving thrust to the subjects like Education/Philosophy, Geography etc. Courses in Management, Banking, Marketing, Commercial Art, T.V. Technology, Computer Science, Electronics, Shorthand and Typing are to be introduced. This will enhance employability of the educated job seekers. The main approach of the manpower planning in the state should be to assist the unemployed to gather work experience/professional skills and to make themselves employable. Motivation and training for self-employment is also necessary otherwise the problem of unemployment will not be solved in the State.

The entire labour force cannot be provided wage paid jobs. It is essential that the unemployed youths entering into the labour market are diverted to take up self-employed professions. A scheme under the central sector has already been started for strengthening the Employment Exchanges for promotion of self-employment by way of providing guidance to the job seekers and to motivate them for diversification from salaries to self-employment ventures. Impact is to be created for awareness amongst the unemployed for taking up self-employment as an alternative to wage/salary paid jobs. Government may therefore take up extension of this programme during the Eighth Plan period and the promotion of self-employment, recognised as one of the important functions of the National Employment Service.

The programme of motivating and guiding job seekers for self-employment may be extended to all the employment exchanges at district level and Sub-divisional level. The employment exchanges should be involved in the selection of beneficiaries under the various self-employment schemes.

The Constitution of India enjoins that, "The state shall take all steps within the limits of its economic capacity for securing the right to work and to public assistance in case of unemployment". In fulfilment of this promise the Government of Assam introduced unemployment assistance scheme. With the assistance, unemployed could be provided with a short relief, but this programme will not generate income and employment. There is a decline in availability of salaried jobs in the organised sector but the number of unemployed is increasing disproportionately. It is in this context that the promotion of self-employment in Assam is necessary. A programme of self-employment for educated unemployed youth (SEEUY) was introduced by the Government of India in 1983-84.

The SEEUY Programme of self-employment is meant for specific target groups (Educated unemployed youth) is quite inadequate to tackle the unemployment problem in Assam. The government also should introduce (SESRU) self-employment for the registered unemployed in Assam.

SERSU has made a considerable impact in the employment position in West Bengal and raised high aspirations of the unemployed youths who have been suffering from frustration because of non-availability of employment in the organised sector.

Important Statistics of Employment

	At the end of		
	Dec. 1986	Dec. 1987	Dec.1988
1. No of applicants registered	223655	168191	166797
2. Vacancies notified to the employment exchanges	13091	13107	10882
3. No. of applicants submitted	154174	145936	104556
4. No. of applicants placed in employment	5241	5538	6347
5. Strength of live register	815251	854415	903702

The self-employment field has got an edge over the wage paid sector in various wages. An unemployed may start a business immediately without waiting for a wage paid job. He is the master of his work. He can create employment, which one wage paid employee can not. His income is indefinite while in wage paid employment the limit is fixed.

Different agencies are now offering self-employment avenues. Agriculture, Veterinary, Fishery, Cooperative, Rural Development, ASIDC, Khadi Board etc., and many other agencies. All are not getting the expected results from these agencies. The reason is due to drop-outs of beneficiaries in the midst of their running ventures. This again due to wrong choice of self-employment avenues by the beneficiaries. In the field of self-employment also, "the motto of matching the right man for the right job holds good".

Before entering into a self-employment venture a prospective beneficiary has to be helped to assess his personal qualities of interest, ability and aptitude in chosen field and also the out turn of the venture chosen. As such proper vocational guidance is a must before entering into the venture.

Different departments may implement their individual self-employment service but the coordination of the vocational guidance section of the National Employment Service is of utmost importance for effective implementation of various self-employment schemes and also to enable the government to have a single window service for reflecting the real statistics about the self-employment schemes and beneficiaries.

As for the labour market information the E.M.I. data has limitations including inadequate coverage and delay in processing. Even though reports are brought out at various levels but these reports are hardly used. The scope of using the data for employment programme has remained unexploited in Assam. In a labour surplus situation the employment exchanges can not serve properly with traditional approaches. The service must reorient the programmes at par with the development needs of the community. In the developing countries the unemployment problem is so deep-rooted in the economy that the employment service can not function as efficiently as in developed countries. Still the employment service should be treated as a basic service like that of a School, Hospital, Post Office, Railway Station as considered in Japan. In Assam also employment promotion programme such as I.R.D.P., N.R.E.P., TRYSEM, have been adopted during the last plan periods. But it has become evident that these programmes are too inadequate to bring any change in the unemployment structure in the state. Moreover, there is no agency in Assam to monitor the employment created by investment made under these programmes in the plan sector.

In a developing state like Assam, the facilities like credit, training, industrial or agricultural extension services have so far remained unutilised and inaccessible to those for whom the services are meant. At the block level there is no good Banking Counter of the nationalised banks and the village unemployed boys or girls do not know anything about the credit facilities to take up self-employment ventures. This has adversely affected the impact of the various credit schemes taken up by the nationalised Banks. The schools also do not have any course to train boys and girls to prepare themselves for credit-worthy activities. The vacuum exists and employment service can step in to fill up this gap.

CHAPTER 6

A Critical Analysis of the Reasons for Unemployment in Assam

The main failure of the Assam's economic planning is the failure to achieve full employment, the failure to eradicate poverty and the failure to create a more equal society and we are discussing the same problem of unemployment today, what we discussed 40 years ago, the First Five-Year Plan. Nehru's formula of the twin Gods of technology and heavy industry have not applied in Assam. Assamese people can cease to be poor only when they can earn adequate income through steady employment all round the year at an adequate level of wages. The major weakness in the planning strategy is that sufficient attention has not been paid to the question of engaging large number of labour in Agriculture. There is no explanation to the reasons for the low utilisation of labour in agriculture, but there is no doubt that fuller utilisation of labour in agriculture offers a durable solution to the problem of rural unemployment.

The large volume of unemployed is having a productive potential capable of creating capital and increasing production, which can eliminate poverty provided they are engaged by creating work opportunities and by channelising the unemployed into productive work. Subsidiaries such as poultry farming, fisheries, dairy farming, afforestation etc. are the best suited areas which need to be scientifically exploited. The Planning Commission has suggested many steps for solution of the unemployment problem. However, even if these policies are implemented, their contribution towards solution of the problem of unemployment and underemployment shall remain and there is serious doubt if the employment target will be reached by the end of the Eighth Plan also.

From time to time the issue of unemployment figured in Parliament. The replies from the Government were that all plans and programmes were employment oriented. Despite such sincerity of purpose, it is rather strange that the problem of unemployment is not solved, rather increasing; but very little concrete facts and figures are available about the extent of unemployment. The information should include categories of unemployment, the centres of unemployment. Sectors where unemployment is prevalent etc. There are figures of unemployment given by the Director General of Employment and Training and the State Directorate of Employment and Craftsmen Training. But these figures mention only about the registered unemployed in the live registers of the employment exchanges. They do not include the lakhs of illiterate people in Assam who do not register with the employment exchanges.

After all the Seven Five-Year Plans in Assam, we have learnt that whatever economic schemes drawn up and implemented in Assam were inadequate to provide employment to the unemployed. The main problem of rural unemployment is the backwardness of the agricultural sector. Infrastructures for greater agricultural productivity through multipurpose cooperative farms on Government waste lands should immediately be created without changing the existing ownership rights of individuals in land. To generate more employment, a labour intensive technology is to be introduced in Assam to absorb the entire manpower surplus thro-ugh all the channels of development. A state wide multipurpose pilot projects for absorbing surplus manpower is necessary for mobilising the unemployed in productive channels and generating the employment potential. In Assam to this day no attempt for absorption of surplus manpower has been made.

In Assam the problem of employment is largely in the

urban areas which is always added by migrants from rural areas and disguised underemployment and low productivity employment in rural areas. Economic activities needed to solve this problem have therefore to be not only aimed at tackling the problem of open unemployment but also that of rural development.

For dealing with the problem of open unemployment the following measures will be more helpful.

Reformation should be brought to the educational system to make it vocationalised at the school level, give it a vocational bias at the undergraduate stage, and admission at the post-graduate level should be restricted to highly qualified persons. Deliberate promotion of low capital intensity in industrial production should be undertaken. Techniques of production that can be undertaken with low capital intensity are to be identified and developed. In order to discourage concentration of unemployed persons in the towns, action should be taken, to promote decentralisation of industrial activity in the rural areas. The nationalised banks should promote small industries in rural areas and encourage self-employment. There should be heavy investment in rural development and application of science and technology in the methods of production followed in rural areas. In the agriculture and non-agriculture activities local capital construction projects such as medium irrigation works, labour intensive methods of cultivation, expansion of animal husbandry, development of other productive activity such as forestry and fishery should be undertaken.

For the underemployed rural farmers there is no way out but to move to nearest towns for non-agricultural works for their employment during the slack period. Action should be taken to find for them year round employment in the rural areas themselves by a policy of rural industrialisation, with a lower average capital intensity. The industrial policy should be for fuller and more effective utilisation of industrial capacity, promotion of labour intensive industrial products. The State employment policy should have the object of giving production employment to the underemployed and unemployed.

There are three major areas of unemployment, the first is the educated urban unemployed including those with specialised education in medicine, engineering or science. The next is the half educated, half skilled rural and urban youths. Most of them will need further training in skills, industrial or agricultural, before they can be employed. In some cases the training can be imparted in service, or under apprenticeship system, but there are not enough institutions, for rural youth to prepare them for the newly emerging jobs and also for self-employed career.

The Apprenticeship Training Scheme under the Apprentice Act, 1961 is being implemented in Assam from 1963. The Apprenticeship Training Act, 1961 was amended in the year 1973 covering the graduates and diplomaholders for Apprenticeship Training under the said Act. The Central Apprenticeship Council is the appropriate authority for implementation of the Apprenticeship Training Scheme in the following organisations.

(a) Any establishment of any Railway, Major port, Mines, Oil fields, or (b) any establishment owned, controlled or managed by (i) the Central Government or a Department of the Central Government, (ii) a company in which not less than 51 per cent of the share capital is held by the Central Government or partly by that Government or partly one or more State Governments. (iii) any Corporation (including Cooperative Societies) established by or under Central Act, which is owned or managed by the Central Government.

In Assam the State Apprenticeship Council or State Council for Technical Education implements Apprenticeship scheme in any establishment other than the establishments specified above.

The State Apprenticeship Council implements the Apprenticeship Training Act in respect of designated trades. The Apprenticeship Act hasfurther been amended and included the technician (vocational) Apprentices under the purview of the said act. Under the Apprenticeship Act, the following seats have located in the State in different Central sector, State and Private sector industries:

The number of located seats:

a. In Central Sector — 844
b. In State Sector — 392
c. In Private Sector — 292

Percentage of utilisation of seats:

a. In Central Sector — 69%

b. In State Sector — 19%
c. In Private Sector — 57%

The short-fall in the utilisation of seats under this scheme may be due to the fact that the Apprentices are not being offered any job on completion of the training in the industries as there is no provision for absorption of Apprentices under the Act, by the employers. Secondly, the Apprentices are not provided with hostel/ housing accommodation during the period of training at or near the industries. Meagre amount of stipend paid to the trade apprentices is not at all sufficient to maintain their expenses including the hiring of accommodation for their lodging near the industry where they are engaged for Apprenticeship Training. Most of the Apprentices including Ex-ITI trainees come from the poor families of rural areas of the State. The existing rates of stipend paid by the employers to the trade apprentices are as follows:

1. 1st Year — Rs. 290/- PM
2. 2nd Year — Rs. 330/- PM
3. 3rd Year — Rs. 380/- PM
4. 4th Year — Rs. 440/- PM

Regarding the absorption of Apprentices it may be stated that a good number of Apprentices, in past, have been absorbed in the Central Sector Industries like ONGC, BRPL, HPC etc. But trend for absorption of the apprentices during the last few years gradually decreased.

The Government of India, in the Ministry of Labour

has kindly offered seats in different trades for Apprenticeship training outside the State. They also recommended for payment of additional amount of stipend over and above the rates of stipend to be paid by the employers. But offer of the Government of India has not been availed of in the State fully.

The recruitment policy also in some of the industries in Assam like Oil India Ltd., Duliajan is dis-advantageous to the Ex-ITI trainees/Apprentices. It is learnt that Oil India Ltd., Duliajan recruits personnel at lower level initially as "Jugali/Khalasi". After 2/3 years of rendering services the said employees are put into test/interview and selected Jugali/Khalasi are engaged as Semi-skilled workers and thereafter the semi-skilled workers again are absorbed in skilled category. Therefore, the Ex-ITI/Apprentices are deprived of such technical posts in different occupations in such industries. The number of apprentices who have successfully completed the training since introduction of the scheme in this State is 1650 upto 1989-90. The position about the regular absorption/employment is not available.

It is important to develop the facilities for skill training which need to be diversified based on local needs. New trades emanating out of modern technology are likely to be in demand in the market should be identified and introduced as part of the training programme. Trades like word-processing, data entry operation and other computer related trades should be introduced for intensive training.

In a backward State like Assam the entire entrants to

the working force cannot be accommodated in the wage paid sector. Whatever may be the pace of industrialisation of the country. It has been accepted that self-employment avenues is the only answer to tackle the ever increasing unemployment problem of the State. If we evaluate at the achievement made in placing the youths of Assam in the self-employment sector, we will find that only a negligible percentage of youths have been able to continue and prosper. Many beneficiaries after obtaining financial help and technical know-how have failed in the chosen field of self-employment. This happens because the beneficiaries do not get proper vocational guidance, before entering into the venture of self-employment. The vocational guidance programme of the employment service which is keeping low now in Assam is to be given greater importance.

The third category of unemployed and underemployed in rural areas are landless labourers, manual workers for whom various programmes of labour intensive rural schemes will have to be implemented, but the right method for implementing those schemes should be to engage local unemployeds or underemployeds. In fact in NREP Schemes also labourers from outside the villages are engaged to construct the roads, embankments etc. in place of local youths. Therefore, the very idea of solving the local unemployment problem through those schemes are defeated. The underemployed or unemployed rural youths shift to the town area seeking employment. To prevent migration of these youths from rural areas to towns, employment generating schemes are to be taken up in the rural area.

Emphasis to be given on intensive cropping, rural development works, self-employment ventures in Agro based occupations such as agriculture, horticulture, sericulture, animal husbandry, fisheries, etc.

Assam has the maximum potential of by products which remained unexplored. This is largely due to lack of proper planning and finance which dragged the State into backwardness in industrialisation. This affects the manpower development and growth of employment.

The main attention therefore should be given to equip the rural youths with necessary technology, besides securing credit, market and other facilities, so that they can start self-employment schemes.

The scope of wage paid employment is directly linked with the expansion of development activities in the public and private sectors. While the public sector cannot provide employment to a rapidly increasing number of job seekers, the private sector has not ex-panded in the State as fast as it should.

While the urban sector is facing the challenge of providing white-collar jobs to the educated, the rural sector is facing the problem of landless farmers/workers, marginal farmers, rural artisans, fishermen etc.

Though agriculture is the primary occupation of the Assamese people, but the Assamese farmers do not know the modern techniques of agriculture. The land is also not utilised fully due to heavy flood in summer and drought in the winter due to lack of irrigation facilities. The most important work is to control the flood and to utilise the water of mightly Brahmaputra for irrigation purpose.

In setting up industries in the public sector in Assam, the authorities always dictate affecting adversely the interest of the local people. Secondly very few of the industries set up in Assam so far are owned by the local entrepreneurs and most of them are owned by people from outside the State.

They do not care to provide employment to the local people in these industries, at least in the responsible posts. They fill up all the key posts with their own people. The local youths get the labourers posts only. Any industrial venture by the local entrepreneurs is sabotaged in the name of competition by the business houses who have their head offices outside the State, and by way of competition and sabotage the local entrepreneurs are eliminated.

Tea, Oil, Timber and Coal industries in Assam are the gifts of British administration. They explored the natural resources of Assam and exported the finished products outside the country for their own economic gain. But British gave Assam a single map of the entire North-East Region bringing Assam in to a single unit of administration. After taking over the administration of Assam the British annexed Cachar, Khasi Jaintia Hills and other hill territories with the British empire, Dimasa Kingdom was annexed in 1854 A.D. The Kuki Naga Kingdom was included in Assam in 1917. In April, 1898 Lushai Hills was annexed.

The British created a single unit of administration in Assam out of the entire North-East Region after establishing capital in Shillong and in 1947 the British administration atleast gave us a map of a great Assam, peace and tranquility. "But during the last 42 years of independence no substantial industrial development have taken place in Assam".

Now Oil, Tea, Coal, Timber industries in Assam are owned by the people from outside the State. In the name of industrialisation they have set up a Toy refinery in Assam of 0.85 MMTPA capacity and diverted the major quantity of crude oil produced from Assam oil fields to set up a major oil refinery of 3.30 MMTPA capacity at Barauni in Bihar to benefit the people of Gangetic valley depriving the Assamese people from their rightful employment in a major oil refinery.

Assam produces 60 per cent of the tea produced in India. But the head offices of all these Tea Companies are located in Calcutta and Assam is deprived of the revenue and taxes earned from her own tea, but major share of the benefit goes to West Bengal. In the tea gardens, the companies appoint Managers from outside the State, only 50 per cent of the Executives are from Assam. The entire economy of Assam is in fact in the hands of non-Assamese people who act against the interest of Assam and the Assamese.

When the Head quarters of Eastern Regional Business Centre of ONGC was established at Nazira in Sibsagar district it was hoped that technical and administrative posts in ONGC will be filled up in the Assam sector by the local candidates. But it is found that the percentage of employment of local qualified candidates in ONGC in 1981 was 75.6 while in 1989 it was 73.0 which indicates that there was a drop in the appointment of local candidates during the period 1981-89. The percentage of employment of outside candidates in Nazira (ONGC) ERSC Head quarters in 1981 was 24.4 while it rose to 27 in 1989. Therefore, it can be observed that the employment policy of ONGC is against the interest of local candidates. The very system of holding interview at Dehra Dun for vacancies at Nazira or any other places in Assam is detrimental to the interest of local candidates. Because it is difficult for unemployed Assamese candidates to travel to Dehra Dun to appear in the interview. Moreover, in many cases it is found that the candidates do not get the call letters in time to appear for the interviews at Dehra Dun. The call letters are posted to them deliberately late. So that the local candidates do not get sufficient time to prepare and go to Dehra Dun to appear in the interviews. The local Assamese candidates are therefore, deprived of job opportunity by any hook or crook by the anti-Assamese lobby in the ONGC. In case of Class I and II officers also the number of local persons are negligible. On 31st March, 1989 out of 2114 Class I officers only 241 i.e., 11.4 per cent were local. This shows that the percentage of Assamese officers in Class I post of ONGC is negligible. Towards this the ONGC authorities forward explanation that there are dearth of local qualified candidates. But Oil India Ltd. which is also an oil industry similar to ONGC in Assam give preference to employment of local candidates from Class I post to downwards and percentage of local officers in Oil India is good. Oil India do not complain that there is dearth of local suitable candidates for Class I post. This argument of ONGC however is not tenable. As on 3-9-90 a total number of 2442 graduate engineers of different disciplines were sitting unemployed since 1986.

The local engineers also are deprived by the Departments and Undertakings. The Calcutta office of the Doordarshan deprived the Assamese engineers in respect of appointments of Engineers at Doordarshan Kendra at Guwahati. Out of 20 Assistant Engineers appointed by the Doordarshan upto 3-9-90 only 6 were from Assam and out of 13 Senior Engineer Assistants 5 were from Assam and out of 19 Engineering Assistants appointed already, 6 were from Assam. The Railway Service Commission at Guwahati for appointments in N.F. Railway was turned into a farce by opening two more recruitment centres at Malda and Patna, to select candidates for the N.F. Railway posts. Many other undertakings like Indian Airlines, Vayudoot, SAIL, HMT etc., has not so far opened any centre for written test in Assam for appointments in those undertakings in Assam. Even in case of appointments in 844 tea gardens in Assam, 579 of them having factories, the local Assamese engineers have so far been deprived. Efforts of many unemployed engineers to start industrial ventures for self-employment failed due to negative attitude of the nationalised Banks towards the local youths, who on the pretext of financial formalities harrass the local youths for years together and finally they are compelled to give up their ventures which are then generally taken up by outside entrepreneurs.

It therefore appears that the employment policy of ONGC and other Departments/Undertakings in Assam sector is not fulfilling the interest of the local unemployed.*

Though we have oil and tea, but these two major industries failed to provide adequate employment to the Assamese unemployed. In the Oil Sector also Assam is not getting justice. Assam is exploited of its own resources.

The total capacity of the existing refineries in Assam i.e., Digboi, Gawahati and Bongaigaon including its expansion programme comes to little over three million metric tones per annum and the capacity of the new refinery proposed at Numaligarh is three million metric tonnes per annum. So the total capacity of all the four refineries in Assam will be around six million metric tonnes per annum. But the crude oil available is estimated at 9 MMTPA in the Eighth Five-Year Plan.

This implies that the excess of 3 MMTPA is going to be pumped out of Assam for refining in the Refineries outside Assam. The capacity of the Barauni Oil Refinary is also being expanded from 3 MMTPA to 4.2 MMTPA. This clearly indicates that the extra 1.2 MMTPA is going to be pumped out from the Assam oil field to Barauni Refinery, though there is scope to expand the local refineries to provide employment to the local unemployees.

---

* *Source*: *The Sentinel*, 31st August, 1990 and the *Assam Tribune*, 4th Sept. 1990.

Men at an age when they are most ambitious if subjected to the humiliation of being unemployed, nothing is more likely to sow seeds of discontentment and consequently this leads to turmoil.

Any number of government jobs will not provide lasting remedy. The objective should be to provide work that is economically productive. The centralisation of industrial production by Delhi in U.P. and Haryana led to concentration of economic power in the hands of U.P. people and unemployment in Assam and other North Eastern States. Decentralisation of industries and investment of capital in small industries over the rural Assam where the workers will work as their own employees and Managers of their own enterprise, will reduce unemployment in Assam.

Authorities have estimated the number of unemployed at 30 per cent of the population and in addition to this there is chronic unemployment during the slack agricultural season.

This is the position of Assam where the first Oil Refinery of the world was set up. The obvious result is the growing discontentment among the employable educated youth, anger, frustration, and damage has already been done to the psychological fabric of the Assamese youths and they are now in turmoil. The most dangerous and distressing implication of the situation is that the large numbers of educated unemployed in their despair have enrolled themselves in many extremist groups.

Unsatisfactory industrial development, a stagnant economy and poverty since independence have caused a sense of deprivation, which is giving rise to fustration and social tension in Assam.

Further the industries located in Assam are guided by profit motive only The resources of the state are being exploited without creating growth of ancillary industries. The tea industry with its more than one hundred years long history in Assam have not made any contribution towards socio-economic development of the state though they are occupying and exploiting the major area of the state's fertile land.

After the discovery of tea in Assam in 1826, the British rulers settled land on specially favourable terms to the planters for cultivation of Tea. "Special waste land grant rules were framed on 6th March, 1838. Under these rules one fourth of the land (grant) was to be held revenue free and on the remaining three-fourth no revenue was to be assessed for the first five years if the land was under grass; ten years if under high grass and twenty years if under forest. On the expiry of the term revenue was assessed nine annas per acre for the next three years after which the rate was fixed for 22 years at the rate of one rupee two annas per acre. The next rules were those of lease hold grants of the 23rd October 1854, under these rules no grant was to be less than 500 acres (afterwards reduced to 200 acres). One-fourth of the grant was exempted from the assessment, the remaining three-fourths were granted revenue free for fifteen years, to be assessed thereafter at 3 annas per acre for ten years and 6 annas an acre for seventy four years more making the whole term for Ninetynine Years lease.

As such large areas of fertile land of Assam was settled with European foreigners in the name of Tea Plantation. These rules were superseded by the simple grant rules issued by Lord Canning in October 1861.

This is the background, how tea plantation in Assam acquired such huge areas of land for tea cultivation at a minimum revenue almost at free of cost which yielded great profit to the planters at the cost of Assamese people from 1826. Whereas Assamese people did not get any employment in these gardens except for a few posts of Male Muhurrirs and Female Muhurrirs. Even the clerks were brought from the undivided Bengal and the Managers were all Europeans. After independence persons from U.P., Haryana and other north Indian states filled up the posts of Managers which have fallen vacant as the European Mangers left the gardens after independece.

The entire labour force in all these gardens are from M.P., Andhra Pradesh and other States. The trade and business in the tea gardens are controlled by people from Rajasthan. It is unfortunate that the unemployed uneducated Assamese youths are not considered for appointment even as labourers in these gardens not to speak of appointment as Managers. As such the Tea Sector has not provided gainfull employment to the Assamese youths and this is one of the main reasons of increasing unemployment in Assam.

The government initiated many employment generating programmes in rural areas. It was during the Third Five-Year Plan that rural employment programmes were initiated. However it was during the Sixth Five-Year Plan that efforts on a large scale was initiated towards provision of employment opportunities in the rural areas. The important programmes are (1) Crash programme, (2) The operation flood diary development project, (3) I.R.D.P., (4) D.R.D.A., (5) TRYSEM, (6) Food for work programme, (7) N.R.E.P., (8) Jawahar Rozgar Yojana etc. But implementation of these programmes have so far not been satisfactory. The programme of employment generation and rual development have suffered from deliberate neglect of rural manpower assessment and planning. The non-vocational education producing graduates who go for white collar jobs only. This is the crux of the problem of unemployment in Assam. Moreover, the half educated rural and urban youths who have either passed matriculation/P.U. or have dropped out of schools are increasing the number of unemployed. As we are still following the old pattern of education, boys and girls after coming out from the schools, colleges, universities in large numbers without any occupational or vocational training do not get any employment in the areas which require skills in par-ticular fields. As such the education system has to be changed to meet the existing situation.

The unemployed youths also cannot take up independent ventures for lack of finances. The Commercial Banks have rather failed to achieve the target, because they are afraid to take the risk on the face of unfavourable recovery. The only State managed financial institutions are Cooperative Apex Bank and the Assam State Cooperative Agriculture and Rural Development Bank are taking lead in financing the unemployed specially the farmers. The Cooperative Apex Bank finances crop loan to the farmers through the Goan Panchayat level societies. But many of the G.P. level societies are not in a position to realise the overdues from the farmers whose crops in the fields have been affected by the successive floods. Consequently, most of the G.P. level societies have lost their eligibility to get finance from the Assam Cooperative Apex Bank. The financial position of the Assam State Cooperative Agriculture and Rural Development Bank is also not good. Many of their branches in the districts have lost their eligibility to get finance from the Head Office, i.e., from the Central Bank due to heavy overdues. The farmers have failed to repay loans taken from this Bank also as their crops have been damaged every year by the successive floods. Therefore for lack of finance, the farmers cannot switch over to multi-crop farming including Rabi crop cultivation in their fields which could enable the farmers to get employment 300 days in a year. As Assam's economy is heavily dependent on agriculture and engage 77 per cent of the total working force of the State. Lack of proper finance also hindering fuller engagement of the available workingforce. *The main problem with Assam is the highest rainfall and the consequent flood for which upto 15 per cent of the cultivated area is inundated every year* by the flood water of the Brahmaputra river. The other constraints are the weakness of the institutions serving the agricultural sector, gaps in policy and absence of systematic planning. Moreover most of the farmers in Assam are on very small holdings. They are following traditional farm practices under rainfed conditions.

Depsite great potential for irrigation in Assam, progress is too slow. Only about 150,000 hectares are under command of surface irrigation. But less than half of the area can be irrigated in the dry season as water management is very poor owing to lack of field channels. The agricultrue sector in Assam has therefore not made much progress during the last 44 years. Over the years from 1965-66 to 1974-75 the total production of food grains increased by 15 per cent whereas during the same period Assam's population increased by 38 per cent. So backwardness in the agriculture sector is the main cause of rural unemployment in Assam.

A large number of registrants are there in the live registers of employment exchanges. But they have not been able to provide employment to them because the employers do not give necessary notification of vacancies to the employment exchanges. Moreover the Staff Selection Commission, the Banking Service Selection Board do not give notification of their vacancies to the employment exchanges for Grade III services. They recruit independently without giving preference to the old registratnts in the employment exhcnages of Assam.

Under the sector of self-employment also the department of employment simply forwards the applications to the District industries centres, who are making necessary enquiry about viability of the projects, recommends the viable cases to the Banking institutions. The department of employment cannot do anything if the Banks do not sanction any loan to the recommended candidates. The provision of C.N.V. Act also do not have any clause to inflict punishment on the defaulters with imprisonment. Therefore the employers do not care even if any cases are filed against them under the C.N.V. Act in Court.

It is well known that the employment exchanges are the main agencies where very large number of unemployed youth gather everyday with the hope of employment assistance, but the scope of which is very limited. The services rendered in the employment exchanges appear hollow, academic and fruitless to the unemployed youths in view of the fact that for getting an employment they have to move to various departments/agencies resulting in avoildable frustration.

Chapter 7

Programmes Implemented by the State Employment Department During Third to Seventh Five-Year Plan to Create Employment in Assam

GENERAL

During the Third Five-Year Plan, an expenditure of Rs. 3.50 lakhs (40 per cent state share) and Rs. 0.12

lakhs (40 per cent state share) in the ad-hoc plan were incurred in setting up of the new Employment Exchanges, Vocational Guidance Units, Professional Executive Office in the State Directorate, Special Employment Exchange for plantation labour, Employment Information and Assistance Bureaux in Rural areas and University Employment Information and Guidance Bureaux at Guwahati and Dibrugarh University to tackle the employment problem of the state.

The Fourth Five-Year Plan schemes under this sector envisage continuance of the measures already undertaken in the plan viz., (i) Expansion of Employment Service, (ii) Collection of Employment Market Information, (iii) Vocational Guidance and Employment Councelling and (iv) Occupational Research and Ana-lysis.

The table below indicates the physical target achieved during the years 1969-70, 1970-71 and 1971-72 and also target for the years 1972-73 and 1973-74.

Item	Unit	Achievement during the year 1969-70 to 1971-72	Target for the year 1972-73 and 1973-74
1	2	3	4
Employment Exchange, U.E.I and G.B. Special Exchange etc.	No	3	3

Contd.

1	2	3	4
Employment Information and Assistance Bureau	No	2	4
Job Development and Industrial Service	No	—	4
Development of Manpower Studies and Research	No	2	3
Development of Vocational Guidance Programme including Occupational Research	No	1	2
Setting up of Publicity Wing in the Directorate and Zones	No	—	5
State Career Study Course	No	—	1
Evaluation and Implementation Unit regarding V.G. Course	No	—	1
Vocational Guidance Officer for School	No	—	4
Career Advice Unit in Colleges	No	—	4

The remaining part of the plan also envisages organisation and restructuring of the employment service which will include (1) strengthening of the employment service to help efficient utilisation of national manpower particularly initial skilled requirement for planned economic growth, and (2) Gearing up the employment service machinery to play a positive role in meeting the manpower requirement of various employment oriented economic development programmes both urban and rural areas.

HILL AREAS

The Fourth Five-Year Plan schemes under this sector envisage continuance of the measures already undertaken in the previous plan and (i) Expansion of Employment Service, (ii) Vocational Guidance and Employment Councellery.

The table below indicate the physical targets achieved during the Third Five-Year Plan and also in the adhoc plans and those proposed for the Fourth Plan.

Item	Unit	Achievement at the end of 1968-69	Proposed for the Fourth Plan
1. Employment Exchanges	No	5	3
2. Employment information and Assistance Bureau	No	6	8

3. Vocational Guidance Emp. Councelling Unit	No	1	4
4. Emp. Market information on unit at the Employment Exchange	No	4	1

The Fourth Plan also envisaged the setting up of an unit at the State Headquarters to deal with Development Schemes in the hill areas and also appointment of Development Officers at the selected exchanges for public relation and promotion of employment service collection of guidance programme will be further intensified during the plan period.

An amount of Rs. 3.00 lakhs have been proposed for implementation of the schemes under employment during the Fourth Year Plan.

FIFTH FIVE-YEAR PLAN

GENERAL

By the end of the Fourth Five-Year Plan, there were 4 zonal offices, 27 employment exchanges including one special employment exchange for plantation labour and three university employment information and guidance bureau, 15 Employment Information and Assistance

Bureau, (2) Collection of Employment Market information units including one State unit and 9 Vocational Guidance units in the state. An enforcement cell for enforcement of the Employment Exchanges (Compulsory Notification of Vehicles) Act, 1959, was set up in the State Directorate during the third year of the Fourth Five-Year Plan.

Stress on the following points have been given in the Fifth Five-Year Plan:

(1) Penetration of Employment Service in the Rural Areas and also strengthening of the existing Employment Information and Assistance Bureau.

(2) Building for the Employment Exchanges.

(3) Vehicles for the Employment Exchanges.

(4) Strengthening of the Employment Exchanges.

(5) Setting up of cells at the Zonal offices for enforcement of Employment Exchanges (Compulsory Notification of Vacancies) Act, 1959.

(6) Setting up of Vocational Guidance units at the Employment Exchange and also strengthening of the existing units.

(7) Setting up of special Guidance centres to cater to the special needs of certain categories of employment seekers e.g., Scheduled Castes/Scheduled Tribes, Ex-servicemen, physically handicapped, Woman etc.

(8) Publicity of activities of the Employment Services.

The estimated expenditure on the implementation of the schemes during the Fifth Five-Year Plan will be Rs. 20 lakhs.

HILL AREAS

By the end of the Fourth Five-Year Plan there will be two Employment Exchanges, Five Employment Information and Assistance Bureaus, two collection of Employment Market Information units and one vocational guidance.

Stress on thc following points have been given in formulation the Fifth Five-Year Plan for the Hill Districts of Assam.

(1) Penetration of Employment Service in the Rural Areas.

(2) Building for the Employment Service in the Rural Areas.

(3) Vehicles for the Employment Exchanges.

(4) Strengthening of the Employment Market Implementation Units of the Employment Exchanges.

(5) Setting up of cells at the Employment Exchanges, for Implementation of the Employment Exchanges (Compulsory Notification of Vacancies) Act, 1959.

(6) Strengthening of the Employment Exchanges.

(7) Strengthening of Vocational Guidance Centres to care to the specific needs of the certain categories of

Employment seekers e.g., scheduled caste/scheduled tribes, Ex-service man, Physically handicapped, woman etc.

(8) Publicity of the activities of the employment service.

The estimated expenditure on the schemes proposed to be implemented during the Fifth Five-Year Plan was Rs. 7 lakhs.

SIXTH FIVE-YEAR PLAN

GENERAL

(a) Brief Review of 1974-75 to 1979-80

During the period between 1974-75 and 1979-80 the following achievement were made:

(1) Two town Employment Exchanges were set up at Nazira and Doom-Dooma.

(2) The professional and executive employment office of the state Directorate were strengthened.

(3) A peripatetic or moving team for street survey, a Research Cell for Employment and Unemployment studies and surveys, state career study course and special cell for SC/ST etc. were set up at State Directorate.

(4) Two Employment Information and Assistance Bureaus were set up one each at Tihu, Barama (Kamrup district) and Katlicherra (Cachar district).

(5) Six Employment Market information units and six Vocational Guidance units were set up in the Employment Exchanges.

(6) The Employment Market Information unit of the District Employment Exchange Guwahati strengthened.

(7) Two rural enforcement cells were set up at Guwahati and Jorhat.

(8) Cell for physically handicapped persons were set up at the State Directorate under the centrally sponsored scheme.

The expenditure during the review was Rs. 10.72 lakhs. Programme for new scheme during 1980-85 (Sixth Five-Year Plan).

(1) Setting up of Employment Exchanges.

(2) Purchase of departmental vehicles for the State Directorate.

(3) Strengthening of the State Directorate by setting up of a departmental vigilance cell.

(4) Setting up of a planning cell at the State Directorate of Employment.

(5) Setting up of a enforcement cell at the zonal officers.

(6) Strengthening of 4 zonal offices in the state at Guwahati, Jorhat, Tezpur and Silchar.

(7) Setting up of Vocational Guidance units at the employment exchange.

(8) Setting up of self-employment cell at the state Directorate.

(9) Strengthening the 3 University Employment Information and Guidance Bureaux during 1983-87.

(10) Setting up of Employment Market Information unit at the Employment Exchange, Doom-Dooma.

(11) Setting up of job Development and Industrial services.

An additional allocation of Re. 1 crore provided during 1980-81 for implementation the schemes on employment for educated youths. After the detailed schemes finalised, amounts were allocated to the concerned departments.

(b) Programme for the Annual Plan 1981-82

During the year 1981-82, proposals have been made for providing Rs. 5.86 lakhs as plan allocation in General Areas under the employment. The amount includes an expenditure of Rs. 4.40 lakhs for meeting the expenditure of the following continuing schemes:

(1) Expansion of Emp. Service	Rs. 155,000/-
(2) Collection of Emp. Market Information	Rs. 124,000/-

(3) Vocational Guidance and Employment counselling	Rs. 133,000/-
(4) Occupational Research and Analysis	Rs. 28,000/-
Total	Rs. 440,000/-

The remaining amount of Rs. 1,45,000/- have been proposed for implementation of the following new schemes during 1981-82 under the major scheme Expansion of Employment Services.

(1) Purchase of a departmental vehicle for the Employment wing of the State Directorate	Rs. 50,000/-
(2) Strengthening of State Directorate of Employment by setting up of a Departmental Vigilance Cell	Rs. 57,000/-
(3) Setting up of a planning cell at the State Directorate of Employment	Rs. 38,000/-
Total	Rs. 145,000/-

HILL AREAS

a. Brief Review of 1974-75 to 1977-80

Out of three existing Employment Exchanges at Diphu, Haflong and Hamren, the Employment Market Information units of the Employment Exchanges at Haflong and Hamren were strengthened and the vocational Guidance unit of the Employment Exchanges, Hamren was also strengthened for rendering better service to Hill tribal applicants. The construction work of the Office building of the Employment Exchange at Diphu and Hamren had been completed and construction of office building of the Employment Exchange at Haflong was started.

b. Proposals for 1981-85

The Employment Service facilities created in the post-plan periods was sustained during the Sixth Plan period. Provision was made for completion of incomplete construction works during the Sixth Plan period. In order to shift the Office of the Hamren Exchange from Donkamokam, residential quarters for the staff will have to be constructed at Hamren where rented accommodation for the staff of the exchange are not available. One more Employment Information and Assistance Bureau at Harangajan in N.C. Hills will be established raising the total number of such unit at Block level to six, Two new Employment Exchanges at Bokajan and Garampani will be opened.

SEVENTH FIVE-YEAR PLAN (1985-90) AND ANNUAL PLAN 1985-86 UNDER EMPLOYMENT

GENERAL

(a) Position of Employment Service at the End of 1979-80 in General Areas

There were 8 District Employment Exchanges, 18 Employment Exchanges, 3 University Employment Information and Guidance Bureaus, 15 Employment Information and Assistance Bureaus, 1 each at the 15 Block development headquarters, 24 Employment Market Information Units, 14 Vocational Guidance Units, 1 Special Employment Exchange for Plantation Labour at Dibrugarh. One special Employment Exchange for Physically Handicapped persons and one professional and executive Employment Office at State Directorate of Employment at Guwahati. There are also 4 zonal offices of the Deputy Director of Employment at Guwahati, Jorhat, Tezpur and Silchar.

(b) Achievements During the Sixth Five-Year Plan (1980-85)

During the year 1980-81, an Employment Exchange for unskilled job seekers had been set up at Guwahati. During the year 1981-82 and 1983-84, it was not possible to implement any new scheme for want of fund.

During the year 1983-84, six Sub-divisional Employment Exchange at Kokrajhar, Goalpara, Borpeta, Mangaldai, Sibsagar and Karimganj have been strengthened and upgraded to the District Employment Exchange for consequent upon creation of 6 new districts in the states 10 new employment exchanges have also been set up one each at (i) Jonai, (ii) Chapakhowa, (iii) Garamur, (iv) Sonari, (v) Biswanath Chariali, (vi) Gosaigaon, (vi) Hatsingimari, (ix) Hojari, (x) Rangia, (xi) Udalguri is consequent upon creation of new sub-divisions.

(c) Programmes for Seventh Five-Year Plan (1985-90)

Objective of Employment Service: The Employment service in the State continued to serve the broad aim of the National Employment service, as has been done over the years through the programmes included in the Seventh Five-Year Plan documents. The objective of these programmes were:

(i) To extend the registration facilities to all sections of the population inhabiting in both urban and rural areas.

(ii) To disseminate information regarding the opportunities offered to the unemployed and underemployed sections of the population by the development activities, more particularly by the activities in the industrial sector in the state and outside.

(iii) To establish liaison between the employment seekers and employers with a view to make a match between job seekers employability and an employers requirement.

(iv) To render vocational guidance to the young people as also seekers regarding choice of career, vocational course and the work of occupations.

(v) To promote as much as possible, self-employing ventures amongst the enterprising unemployed youth through motivation, counselling and guidance.

(vi) To collect, process and disseminate employment in the different fields of economic activities for the benefits of employers, job seekers and manpower planners.

(vii) To improve working necessary accommodation component and manpower for implementation of the different schemes including schemes taken up for the benefits of the seekers such as physically handicapped persons, scheduled castes and scheduled tribes applicants and women job seekers.

To achieve the objective mentioned above, schemes for the following are considered essential for inclusion in the Seventh Five-Year Plan.

FORMULATION OF DRAFT SEVENTH FIVE-YEAR PLAN (1985-90) AND ANNUAL PLAN 1983-84 UNDER EMPLOYMENT (HILL AREAS)

Position of Employment Service at the End of 1979-80 (Fifth Five-Year Plan)

There were 3 Employment Exchanges at Diphu, Haflong and Hamren in Hill areas at the end of 1979-80. There were also 3 Employment Market Information units and 3 Vocational Guidance units, one each at the aforesaid Employment Exchanges. There were also employment information and Assistance Bureaux including 3 in Karbi Anglong district and 2 N.C. Hills district.

During 1980-81, a post of Deputy Director of Employment (Hills) was created together with one class III and class IV staff with the headquarters at Diphu for liaison and supervision of the work in Employment Exchanges in the two hill districts. One post of LDA was created in the district Manpower Planning and Employment generation councils of the District Employment Exchange, Haflong 1983-84.

(a) Programme for Seventh Five-Year Plan (1985-90)

Objective of Employment Service: The Employment Service in the state will continue to serve the broad aim of the National Employment Service, as has been done over the years, through the programme included in the Seventh Five-Year Plan document. The objectives of these programmes will be:

PART I

(i) To extend the registration facilities to all sections of the population inhabiting in both urban and rural areas.

(ii) To establish liasion between the employment seekers and employers with a view to making a match between a job seekers employability and employers requirement.

(iii) To promote as much as possible, self-employing ventures amongst the enterprising unemployed youth through motivation, counselling and guidance.

(iv) To improve working of the Employment service by providing necessary accommodation, equipment and manpower for implementation of the different schemes including schemes taken up for the benefit of the weaker sections such as the Scheduled Castes and Scheduled Tribes applicants.

To achieve the objective set above, schemes for the following considered essential for inclusion in the Seventh Five-Year Plan:

PART II

(i) It was proposed to establish 2 new Employment Information and Assistance Bureaux under Hill areas plan, to be located in the interior Rural areas as also growth centres.

(ii) The directions contained in the Sixth Plan for promotion of self-employment amongst the enterprising unemployed youth has not yet been properly implemented in absence of the necessary staff in the

Employment Generation Councils have been set up in the two District Employment Exchanges. The proposed unit consisting of the Assistant Employment Officer, one Lower Division Assistant and one peon in each of these two District Employment Exchanges will function as the Secretariat of the District Councils in the matter.

(iii) Almost all the Employment Exchanges in the state are now accommodated in the hired buildings and accommodations is not available in the interior areas even for the purpose of hiring. With a view to giving a better look to the Employment Services, it has been proposed to have employment Exchange buildings and staff quarters as per the layout of the Directorate General of Employment and Training, New Delhi.

ACHIEVEMENT DURING THE SEVENTH FIVE-YEAR PLAN UPTO END OF 1988-89

During the year 1985-86:

(i) Strengthening the 8 District Employment Exchanges—Guwahati, Jorhat, Tezpur, Dibrugarh, Silchar, North Lakhimpur, Nagaon and Dhubri by setting up of 8 units of District Manpower Planning and Employment Generation Councils by creation of 8 posts of Asstt. Employment Officers, 8 posts of L.D. Asstt. and 8 posts of peon.

ii) Upgradation of the Sub-Divisional Employment Exchange, Nalbari by creation of post of Employment Exchange Officer, one U.D. Asstt., Three L.D. Asstts. and two peons.

(iii) Strengthening the state Employment Market Information unit by creation of a post of Statistical Asstt. During the year 1986-87, (1) Assam Zone, Guwahati by creation of a post of chowkidar, (2) Strengthening the zonal offices of the Dy. Director of Employment at Guwahati, Jorhat, Tezpur and Silchar by creation of four posts of L.D. Asstt., one post of L.D. Asstt., four each zonal offices of the Dy. Directors of Employment, (3) Strengthening the Zonal Offices of the Dy. Director of Employment at Tezpur and Silchar by Setting up of 2 enforcement cells for enforcing the compulsory Notification of Vacancies Act, 1959 with creation of two posts of Asstt. Director of Employment (Enf.), two L.D.A. and two peons. One Asstt. Director of Employment (Enf.), one L.D.A. and peon in each of the two Zonal Offices of the Dy. Director of Employment, (4) Setting up of an Employment Exchanges, one each at Jagiroad, Moranhat and Patharkandi by creation of three Asstt. Employment Officers, three U.D. Asstts., six L.D. Asstts., six peons and three chowkidars, (5) One zonal office of the Dy. Director of Employment at Dibrugarh was set up with one Dy. Director of Employment, Two L.D. Asstts. one peon and one chowkidar, (6) One coordination cell for the District Manpower Planning and Employment Generation Council was set up in the State Directorate by creation of Dy. Director of Employment, one Investigator, two L.D. Asstts. and one peon during the year, 1987-88, (7) Setting up of 7 units of Employment Market Information in the 7 Employment Exchanges at Rangia, Gossaigaon, Hatsingimari, Udalguri, Viswanath, Chariali, Sohari and Hojai by creation of 7 posts of Statistical Asstts. and 7 posts of L.D. Asstts., one statistical Asstt. and one L.D. Asstt. in each of these 7 units, (8) Setting up of 2 Employment Exchanges, one each at Koliabor and Duliajan by creation of two Asstt. Employment Officers, two U.D. Asstts., Four L.D. Asstts., two peons and two chowkidars, (9) Setting up of 3 Vocational Guidance and Employment Councelling units and strengthening one V.G. unit at the District Employment Exchange, Barpeta by creation of four posts of Asst. Employment Officers, three L.D.As. and 3 peons. (10) Setting up of the four Employment Information and Assistance Bureau one each at the Block Devt. Headquarters at Bijni in Kokrajhar District, Dhakuakhana in Dhemaji Sub-Division by creation of 4 posts of U.D. Asstts., (11) Strengthening the Five District Employment Exchanges at Barpeta, Kokrajhar, Goalpara, Mangaldai, and Sibsagar by setting up of 5 units of District Manpower Planning and Employment General Council with creation of 5 Asstt. Employment Officers, 5 L.D.As. and 5 peons, one Asstt. Employment Officer, one L.D.As. and one peon in each of the five units, (12) Setting up of a Mobile Employment Exchange attached to the state Directorate by purchasing one Mini Bus. (13) Setting up of four units of Employment Information and Assistance Bureau in the 4 Devt. Block Headquarters at Rupahi in Barpeta district, Bajali Chowkathi in Barpeta district, Bakakhat in Golaghat district and Demow in Sibsagar district. Setting up of an Employment Exchange at Dhansiri Subdivision in the headquarter at Sarupather. Strengthening the Mobile Employment Exchange attached to the State Directorate.

HILL AREAS

ACHIEVEMENT DURING THE SEVENTH FIVE-YEAR PLAN

1985-86

A. Expansion of Employment Service

(1) Strengthening of the Employment Exchange at Bokajan and Garampani by creation of a post of U.D. Asstt. and one peon for each Employment Exchange	No	2	Achieved

B. Vocational Guidance and Employment Counselling

(1) Strengthening of the Dist. Manpower planning

and Employment Generation Council of the District Employment Exchange, Diphu by creation of a post of L.D.A.	No	1	Achieved
C. Construction of office building of the 3 offices, quarters for the District Employment Exchange, Hailong	No	2	10% of the works achieved

1986-87

A. Expansion of Employment Service

(1) Setting up of an Employment information and Assistance Bureaux at Haranganjan in N.C. Hills	No	1	Achieved
B. Construction of 3 Officers quarters of the District Employment Exchange, Haflong	No	1	20% of the work achieved

1987-88

A. Expansion of Employment Service

(1) Strengthening of the office of the Dy. Director of Empl. Diphu by creation of a post of LDA and one Chowkidar	No. 1	Achieved
(2) Construction of 3 officers Qrs. of the Dist. Emp. Exchange Haflong	No. 1	20% of the work achieved

1988-89

(1) Construction of 3 Officers Qrs. of the Dist. Employment Exchange, Haflong	No. 1	work-in-progress
(2) Construction of one officers quartes and one retaining wall of the Dist. Employment Exchange, Diphu	No. 2	Govt. sanction received PWD have been been requested to start the work without delay

PROGRAMME FOR THE EIGHTH FIVE-YEAR PLAN

Altogether Rs. 598.21 lakhs are proposed for the Eighth Five-Year Plan period. Out of these Rs. 235.11 lakhs would be required for maintenance of the establishment cost of the continuing schemes including continuing construction works. The rest will be invested in the new schemes.

The position of unemployed educated youth in Assam after the end of the Seventh Five-Year Plan are as follows:

(A) Total number of unemployed registered youths with Masters Degree, Graduate, P.U., and H.S.L.C. passed in the State upto December, 1989 are as follows:

i)	Masters Degree holders	—	4088
ii)	Graduate	—	61018
iii)	P.U. passed	—	117333
iv)	H.S.L.C. passed	—	351305

(B) Total number of Masters degree holder, Graduate, PU passed and H.S.L.C. passed applicants who got Employment through Employment Exchanges during the period of A.G.P. i.e. from 1986 to December 1989 are as follows:

i)	Masters Degree	—	82
ii)	Graduate	—	1785
iii)	P.U. passed	—	3793

(C) Data in case of Linguistic minorities and Ex-Tea garden labourer are not collected. Total number of Religious Minorities, Scheduled Castes and Scheduled Tribes applicants got employment during the period from 1986 to 1989 are as follows:

(i)	Religious Minorities	—	2181
(ii)	Scheduled Castes	—	1663
(iii)	Scheduled Tribes	—	2401

The total strength of Live Register of Educated applicants in the state at the end of December, 1989 was 5,52,215.

The Live Register of some special categories of applicants in the state at the end of December are as follows:

(a)	Scheduled Castes	—	56750
(b)	Schedule Tribes	—	89472
(c)	Ex-Servicemen	—	2587
(d)	Physically handicapped	—	2993
(e)	Women	—	171196

The strength of total Live Register of the Employment Exchange in the state as on 31.12.89 was 9,77,126.

Source: Directorate of Employment and Craftsmen Training, Assam, Guwahati.

CHAPTER 8

Recommendations

On his first visit to Assam in 1921, Gandhiji expressed the views that "Every woman of Assam is a born weaver. She weaves fairy tales in cloth. No Assamese girls who does not weave can expect to become a wife. The home industries are flourishing in Assam and there is good prospect for spinning and weaving. Nature is bountiful and pressure of population is not felt".

When Sardar Vallabhbhai Patel visited Assam in 1948 in the capacity as Deputy Prime Minister observed "Your's is a land for Gods to live in. Its air, its natural scenery, its pure atmosphere, its sweet water will attract even Gods, you have then to harness your rivers".

Late Gopinath Bordoloi pleaded before the cabinet mission that Assam must have full control of all her resources subject to some suitable contribution for maintenance of the centre.

Dr. Rajendra Prasad came for the first time to Assam in 1922. Two years later he re-visited Assam. His third visit took place when he came to Assam to attend the session of the Indian National Congress in 1926. He also paid a visit to Assam as the President of the Indian Republic in 1950 to console the people of Assam who suffered a great earthquake on 15th August, 1950. After his visit he wrote that "In Assam rearing Eri, Muga and spinning yarn out of them widely prevalent. The woman folk of Assam are expert weavers.

A girl of a good family is not given in marriage if she is not accomplished in weaving and spinning. They know to weave cloth of various designs and colour in their own looms. Almost every family possesses a loom and a Charkha".

During the medieval period also weaving was most important under the Ahom and Koch Rulers. Cultivation was done vigorously in the country. But towards the last part of Ahom Rule, the conditions of the Assamese cultivators became very miserable. The Moamaria revolt and the Burmese invasions were responsible to a great extent for the fall in the cultivation in Assam. Although there was no project for irrigation, yet it cannot be said that people were ignorant for irrigating their fields. "Robinson" admits the existence of the practice of field irrigation. People were accustomed to the construction of embankments called *"Mathauri"* along the banks of the rivers to check the rushing water of the rivers into the fields during flood.

Mr. B.C. Allen observed on the activities of the Ahom King (Assam District Gazetters Vol. VI, B.C. Allen, 1905 p. 41) that embankments constructed along the side of some of the rivers near the capital protected land which became uncultivable. Embankments of this nature were constructed along the left Bank of the Brahmaputra from Silghat to Kajlimukh. While constructing the embankment during the period of Ahom Kings, local Assamese labourers were employed. But now-a-days, all the labourers engaged in construction works of Mathauries are labourers from Bihar.

Local labour is not engaged by the contractors and this fact is known to all including the Indian leaders right from 1922. [In fact, when Dr. Rajendra Prasad visited Assam in 1922 for organisational work of the Congress Party, he had to go to the remote villages in Bullock Carts through jungles, he found that in Assam villages, Bihari porters were working. The carters were all Biharies. While taking his bath in Brahmaputra river, he saw Boatmen were from Chapra District in Bihar. This sweet-meat vendors in the steamers were all from Bihar].*

---

* *Source*: [(English version from Dr. Rajendra Prasad's Autobiography (In Hindi) *Mere Atmakatha*) collected from discovery of Assam by Sri Satish Kakoti].

From the above observations of Dr. Rajendra Prasad also, it appears that all these works in the Small Scale Sector were taken over by the Biharies from the Assamese people before 1922. Dr. Rajendra Prasad further observed that under the prevailing laws it was easy for any person to settle in Assam and acquire land. People from Maymansing District of the then undivided Bengal came to Assam and reclaimed the fallow lands. They acquired rights over the land, in this way the immigrant population (from Bangladesh) in Assam inflated gradually occupying the vast areas of farm land making the Assamese farmers owners of fragmented small holdings, over which he and his dependents cannot engage themselves throughout the year, and this is the main cause of the resultant growth of under employment in the Agricultural Sector in Assam.

In the Industrial Sector, the new Industrial Policy of Assam was announced in December, 1986 with special emphasis on optimum utilisation of locally available raw materials, with wider avenues of employment to local people, development of manpower and technical skill. Stress has been laid on development of labour intensive sector of small scale and village industries. The new policy plans to generate employment of local people through setting up of industries, based on locally available raw materials. The Industrial Employment Policy is framed in such a way as to safeguard the interest of the local people. Employment reservation to the local people, 100 per cent for the small sector, 80 per cent in the managerial and 90 per cent in non-managerial cadres for the medium sector which has to fulfil this provision within five years of the establishment of the industry. The concessions and incentives will be denied to those units which will fail to observe this employment policy. But it is preposterous to have such an industrial policy without defining the term local people. It is unfortunate that the term 'local people' has not been precisely defined by the authorities and for this the industrial policy so far has not come to any help to the local people and outsider industrialists are taking advantage of the failure on the part of the authorities to define the term local people to their benefit by unscrupulous methods.

This region of the country has the maximum potential by products which remained unexplored. This is largely due to perhaps lack of proper planning and finance which dragged the entire Assam into backwardness in the field of industrialisation. This has not only affected the growth of employment and manpower development in proper direction but also affected the total economy of the region.

In Assam as per the information recorded in the live registers of the Employment Exchanges, the unemployment position as on 31-12-89 stood as follows:

1. Total number in live Registers	9,77,126
2. Total number of Educated applicants	5,52,215
3. Total number of Unskilled applicants	4,24,911
4. H.S.L.C/Matric passed	3,51,305
5. H.S.S.L.C./P.U. passed	1,17,333

6. Graduates	61,018
7. Post-Graduates	4,088
8. Passed out ITI Trainees	12,622
(a) Engg. Trade	11,395
(b) Non-Engg. Trade	1,227
9. Engineering Graduates	1,416
10. Medical Graduates	254
11. Agricultural Graduates	120

The total number of job seekers in the live registers shoot up from 3,60,343 in May, 1981 to 8,32,426 in May, 1987. The educated unemployed in the live registers shoot up from 1,49,799 in 1981 to 4,51,938 in July, 1987. Out of them, over 50 per cent were matriculates or above. Only 3.5 per cent of the registrants got a chance of placement every year. While the rest continue their search for jobs. The process of development have not generated employment for the educated people in comparison to the supply from various educational institutions.

The scope of wage paid employment is directly linked with the expansion of the development activities in the public and private sectors. But public sector alone cannot provide employment to the highly increasing number of job seekers. In the State of Assam the Private Sector has not extended to the desired extent. Therefore, the employment policy of the State should give more importance to self-employment.

Generation of employment in the self-employment sector will mainly depend on provision of credit, supply of raw materials and marketing support. Such schemes will prevent migration of rural labour to the urban areas in search of white-collar jobs.

Emphasis should be given on intensive cropping, rural development programmes, extension of the knowledge of scientific cultivation to the small farmers. Centres should be opened for maintenance of farm equipment and Agro-machineries in the villages. One window of Farmers Agro-Service Centres also should be opened in the Central Villages. Agro based and water based small village industries should be started.

In the urban sector, to attract the unemployed to the self-employment schemes; programmes on entrepreneurial development should be launched. District Industries Centres should provide new entrepreneurs all support that are available under the new industrial policy.

Credit is an absolute must for the self-employment schemes. Govt. may make provisions for easy loans through State Financial Institutions as the Commercial Banks do not sanction loans easily. The District Industries Centres should keep coordination with the employment officers and they should give first preference to the candidates recommended by the employment exchanges and ensure that the beneficiaries are the seniormost registrants of the employment exchanges.

The State Development Departments including the P.W.D., E & D, Irrigation etc. should entrust all their works to the local Assamese contractors with conditions that they must engage local labourers in the works.

Eri, Muga rearing, spinning and weaving should be organised on a large scale on cooperative basis.

Consequent on the formulation of a policy to provide self-employment, the Government of India selected 32 employment exchanges in the country. The District Employment Exchange, Guwahati was one of them. A self-employment promotion cell was opened at Guwahati and it started functioning from 1st February, 1984. Since then it has been assisting those unemployed youths who are interested to start their self-employment ventures. Similar services are also being rendered by the District Employment Exchanges of other districts having manpower planning and employment generation councils. But there is no provision of its own for sanctioning seed money or subsidy to registered unemployed youths, the role of the employment exchanges in this regard continues to be confined to motivation and identification of entrepreneurs and providing linkage services. Financial assistance plays a vital role in the successful implementation of the self-employment programme.

Experience of the past few years reveals that the registered unemployed youths have taken indifferent attitude towards the employment exchanges due to their limitations in financial aspect of the programme.

A large number of unemployed youths gather everyday in the employment exchanges with the hope of assistance, the scope of which is very limited in the employment exchanges. The services rendered at the employment exchanges appears hollow, academic and fruitless to the unemployers, in view of the fact that for achieving the results of guidance and motivation given by the employment exchanges, the candidates have to move to various departments/agencies resulting in avoidable frustration in many cases. Selection, motivation, guidance as well as rendition of required financial assistance from a single counter is a concept which seems to be less failure prone than the present system. The prevailing frustration of the unemployed youths towards employment exchanges in establishing their proposed self-employment ventures mainly for approaching many departments can be minimised if such services can be rendered at the exchange premises.

In order to obviate the difficulties in implementing the self-employment programme by the employment exchanges, a scheme should be introduced to provide seed money/subsidy to the eligible registered unemployeds in Assam on the lines being followed in the States of Jammu and Kashmir, U.P., Maharashtra and Kerala. The Government of West Bengal also introduced a similar scheme to assist the unemployed young men and women registered with the employment exchanges of West Bengal to be financed by the Scheduled Commercial Banks with a provision of 25 per cent subsidy as sanctioned project cost from the State Government through the Employment Exchanges. In Assam also Govt. may examine the matter and take steps to introduce a self-employment scheme for the registered unemployeds of Assam on the line as introduced by the Government of West Bengal.

West Bengal Government have already started a scheme on self-employment known as "SESRU" from 1985-86 financial year. Upto 1989, West Bengal Government have been able to start around 60,000 self-employment projects under "SESRU" sanctioned by banks and the West Bengal Financial Corporation. The total value of the projects sanctioned upto the end of 1989 was of the order of Rs. 105 crores. The State Government incurred expenditure of Rs. 26 crores on account of 25 per cent margin money grant. A large number of unemployed and underemployed persons could be assisted for self-employment in West Bengal under "SESRU".*

In Assam also such self-employment schemes on the pattern of "SESRU" of West Bengal should be introduced. 50 per cent of the expenditure to be met as margin money should be given by the Central Government to the State Government as matching grant and if we implement such self-employment schemes in Assam at least 50 per cent of the unemployed will be engaged in self- ventured vocations which will definitely bring a ray of hope to the young talents who are now in turmoil in Assam.

The State Government should create market for Eri/Muga products in the foreign markets and take up export of Eri/Muga products in a bigger scale. The Polyester Fabric produced in the B.R.P.L. shall have to be

---

* *Source*: (Address by Sri Santi Ranjan Ghatak, Labour Minister of West Bengal to the delegates of 28th meeting of the Working Group on National Service held at Siliguri on 8-10-89).

utilised by motivating the traditional handloom weavers to switch over to polyester weaving providing them with the technical knowledge of such weaving. The Sericulture and Weaving Department should popularise remodelled looms and motivate traditional weavers to switch over to polyester weaving. Rural youths should be encouraged and motivated to start farming on commercial lines to take up diary farming, poultry farming, piggery etc.

The manpower division of the Planning and Development Department should ensure continuous flow of information of current and future demand and supply of personnel in different occupations. The manpower division should work out the skilled manpower requirement, then identify the institutions which will impart the required training. The proposed Oil Refinery at Numaligarh, the Gas Cracker Project, would require the services of trained personnel in various fields. Moreover, the introduction of computerisation in different public and private sector industries, Railways, Post Offices, Banks, there is demand for skilled manpower. It is therefore necessary that the local youths are to be trained in computerisation so that trained local youths can be employed in these sectors. All vocational and technical courses in the ITIs, Polytechnics and Engineering Colleges will have to be diversified so as to make them more relevant to the requirement of technical personnel in the state.

The applicants with general qualifications constitute about 80 per cent of the total unemployed and more than 50 per cent of the educated unemployed in Assam.

These unemployed youths can only be absorbed in Government offices and public undertakings as Assistants, Typists, Teachers etc.

But there is excess supply of candidates than demand for such posts. Hence, there is shortage of employment for those candidates. In the private sector, the employer always tries to recruit best talents and do not employ incompetent persons. They, therefore, recruit persons from the open market (outsiders) to meet their demand. Government therefore, through the State Directorate of Technical Education should standardise the training in the various vocational institutes and ensure that the training imparted in these institutes are of a very good standard and after completion of training in these institutes, the candidates become more competent and can go through any competitive examination taken for recruitment of persons by any employer.

The provisions of the employment exchanges (Compulsory Notification of Vacancies) Act, 1959 and rules framed thereunder should be strictly enforced in the state.

Restriction should be imposed on all industries to recruit and fill up 100 per cent of the vacancies in their establishments out of the local candidates, because now there is no dearth of local candidates in any trade or skill, failing which their licences should be cancelled. State Government must ensure that Tea, Oil, ONGC shift their Head Offices including the recruiting Centres to Assam. State Government should establish one institute of Oil/Tea Technology in Assam with a Five Year

Degree Course and make compulsory that all the Tea Gardens/Oil/ONGC in Assam must appoint the candidates on managerial posts after their successful completion of the course. The institute may be affiliated with the Dibrugarh University as major number of the Tea Gardens and Oil fields in Assam are located in Upper Assam Zone.

The Secondary Education should be vocationalised. The Education Department should evaluate the curriculum of introducing computer training in the Secondary Education in Consultation with AMTRON (Assam Electronic Development Corporation Ltd.).

The course of education are so framed that the students are not equipped with any productive skills whatever education they receive cuts them off from their natural and social environment. It converts them into a parasitic class which intensify the poverty of the masses. It is clear that the present system of education has outlived its utility whatever it ever had.

Only vocationalisation of Secondary Education can provide valuable manpower for economic growth. The salient features of vocationalisation are the following:

1. Enhancement of individual employability; reduction of mismatch between he demand and supply of skilled manpower and provisions of alternatives for those pursuing higher educations without particular interest or purposes.
2. Vocational educations are to be a distinct stream intended to prepare students for identified occupations.

3. Development of attitudes, knowledge and skills for entrepreneurship and self-employment.

Training Centres should be arranged by the State Employment Department for jobs in Railways, Banks, other Financial Institutions, Telephones, Telecommunications etc. The Employment Department also should arrange training for jobs like Sales representative, Company Secretary, Chartered Accountant as there has been increase in the demand for such jobs.

The above recommendations, if implemented will reduce the problem of unemployment in Assam to a limited extent only. Full employment will depend on the success of self-employment generation and making productive labour, based on which one can keep building his career.